ACKNOWLEDGMENTS

Editor Francesca Coles would like to acknowledge the following people for their contributions to this phrasebook:

Martin Hughes for writing the appropriately irreverent and jaunty text and for providing insights into the 'damnable and delightful' country that is Ireland past and present. Martin was born, raised and quartered in Dublin where, as an adult, he dithered for several years between journalism and public relations. In the grand old Irish tradition, he left in search of even greener pastures, travelling for three years before settling in Melbourne, Australia. He totally missed out on the Celtic Tiger and Ireland's economic boom but is not bitter.

Gerry Coughlan for providing the bulk of the Irish English words and phrases in this book. Gerry grew up in Dublin but emigrated to the bog end of Africa (Johannesburg, South Africa) before U2 and Riverdance made it big. He works behind the scenes in the arts and entertainment industry and has a popular website called Everyday English and Slang in Ireland at www.irishslang.co.za. Gerry was inspired to create the site after reading a few Roddy Doyle novels and being reminded of many delightful Irish turns of phrase that he'd almost forgotten.

Many thanks also to Fionn Davenport for his help, and to expatriate in-house Irishman and editor Cahal McGroarty for his Irish language expertise in providing transliterations and comments on the Irish-language material and for willingly answering countless queries.

Lonely Planet Language Products

Publishing Manager: Chris Rennie
Commissioning Editors: Karin Vidstrup Monk & Ben Handicott
Editor: Francesca Coles
Assisting Editor: Vanessa Battersby
Layout Designer: Jacqui Saunders & David Kemp

Cartographer: Wayne Murphy
Project Manager: Adam McCrow
Managing Editor: Annelies Mertens
Acting Layout Manager: Kate McDonald
Series Designer: Yukiyoshi Kamimura

KT-467-747

Acknowledgments

3

Irish
Language & Culture

Irish Langu...
1st edi...

...ely Planet Publications Pty Ltd ABN 36 005 607 983
90 Maribyrnong St, Footscray, Victoria 3011, Australia

Lonely Planet Offices
Australia Locked Bag 1, Footscray, Victoria 3011
USA 150 Linden St, Oakland CA 94607
UK 72-82 Rosebery Ave, London, EC1R 4RW

Cover
Irish montage by Yukiyoshi Kamimura
© Lonely Planet Publications Pty Ltd 2007

ISBN 978 1 74059 577 3

text © Lonely Planet Publications Pty Ltd 2007

10 9 8 7 6 5 4 3 2

**Although the authors and Lonely Planet try to make the infor-
mation as accurate as possible, we accept no responsibility
for any loss, injury or inconvenience sustained by anyone
using this book.**

Republic of Ireland and Northern Ireland

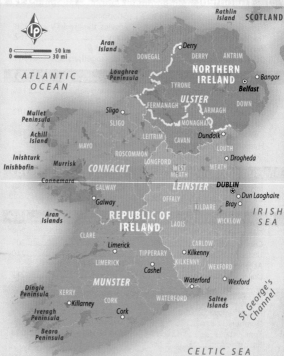

An Gaeltacht (Irish-speaking areas)
Republic of Ireland
- Connacht
- Leinster
- Munster
- Ulster (R.I.)

Northern Ireland
- Ulster (N.I.)

Introduction

Ah, Ireland … that damnable, delightful country, where everything that is right is the opposite of what it ought to be.
—Benjamin Disraeli

Of all their national traits, characteristics and cultural expressions it's perhaps the way the Irish speak and write that best distinguishes them. Indeed, scattered all over the globe by hardship, oppression and these days just for kicks, the Irish have had to ingratiate themselves in many foreign lands. You have to wonder if they'd have done so well if it wasn't for the lilting eloquence of their speech and their easy, mischievous charm – a direct result of how they speak.

For all their funny accents, the Irish are masters of the English language, or at least their version of it. They're generally confident orators, have excellent elocution and like nothing more than a good debate (preferably over a pint). It's for this reason that thousands of foreign students flock to Irish shores every summer to study English. Well, come on, it certainly wouldn't be the weather that attracts them, would it?

How English is spoken in Ireland (a language known by scholars as Hiberno-English and in this book as Irish English) is the result of almost a millennium of struggle between the native Irish and the marauding English tongue. It's a linguistic record of the clash between Irish and English cultures that's taken place ever since the Anglo-Normans came to Ireland for their holidays in the 12th century (and ended up staying on) and particularly since the *Plantations* (of Irish lands by English lords) from the late 16th century.

Introduction

7

When cultures clash, the oppressed inevitably learn the language of their oppressors and so it's gone in Ireland for centuries. Despite being pushed to the margins and preserved as a first language in only a few remote parts of Ireland known as the **Gaeltacht** (pronounced *gayl·takht)*, the Irish language (from now on referred to simply as 'Irish') grafted itself onto the local version of English by imposing its rhythms, pronunciation patterns and grammatical peculiarities.

This hybrid quality is what makes Irish English unique. Touching the tip of the iceberg, have you ever noticed how the Irish rarely give straight 'yes' or 'no' answers? It goes against their instincts because there are no direct translations of either word in Irish. This avoidance of monosyllabic answers just might be part of the reason it's so easy to strike up a conversation with an Irish person.

Another example of Irish influence on Irish English is in the area of pronunciation. The sound system of Irish doesn't allow for an *s* sound before a *t*, an *n* or an *l*, opting instead for a *sh* sound. The influence of this pronunciation rule is still felt in the Irish English spoken in the west of Ireland where, for example, the word 'strike' is pronounced 'shtrike'. So it's not that they've no discipline when it comes to pronunciation, it's just that, thanks to Irish, they play by a different set of rules. The influence of Irish is also why you'll often hear characteristic forms such as **he's after going to the shops** (meaning 'he's just gone'), which have been incorporated into Irish English based on Irish grammatical models.

The linguistic impact of the contact between Irish and English is most clearly preserved in the prose and dialogue of Irish writers and playwrights from the early 20th century, particularly Sean O'Casey and JM Synge. These writers eloquently captured the language and vernacular of the working-class Irish people at a time when the battle between the English and Irish languages was still, perhaps literally, ringing in their ears. The impact can also be gauged in those areas where Irish is still spoken as a mother tongue or where it has survived until recently. Dialects of Irish English in **Gaeltacht** regions diverge most markedly from Standard English.

The second-biggest influence on modern Irish English came, not so much from the conflict between English and Irish but from the historical links between Scotland and Ulster (see the section on Ulster English, page 17).

You'll be a richer person for experiencing Irish English and this humble little book (that's Irish modesty) will be your trusty companion as you begin your voyage of discovery (that's Irish *blarney*).

CELTIC ROOTS

The Iron-Age warriors known as the Celts, who arrived on Irish shores from Eastern Europe around 500 BC, could not have imagined the far-reaching impact they'd have on their little island home. The Celtic language they brought with them (known as *Goidelic*) formed the basis of what's known as *Primitive Irish*. The first record of this language comes from inscriptions in the *Ogham* alphabet on stone monuments up to about the 4th century. More than 300 of these inscriptions have been found in Ireland (and many more have been discovered in areas of the Celtic diaspora for the period like Scotland and Wales). They provide valuable insights into the evolution of the language which came to be known as Irish. *Primitive Irish* evolved into *Old Irish* (from the 6th to the 10th centuries) which gave way to *Middle Irish.* The language assumed its contemporary *Modern Irish* form in the 16th century.

THE VIKINGS BRING BEER

Norsemen, or Vikings, came to Ireland in the 10th century and had a significant influence on Irish culture and language. In keeping with their areas of expertise, they gave the local language many seafaring and commercial terms. These invaders liked the place so much they eventually assimilated into the local culture. In doing so they provided many important place names, such as Waterford, which came from the Norse word *Vedrarfjord* 'windy fjord', and Leixlip in County Kildare, which stems from the Norse *laxhlaup* 'salmon leap'. Curiously, they also donated words for many domestic objects (perhaps a measure of just how much they felt at home). The most important donation was the word *bjorr*, which became **beoir** (pronounced byor) in Irish and just plain 'beer' in English.

ANGLO-NORMANS INTRODUCE ENGLISH

When the Anglo-Normans hit the country (in more ways than one) in the 12th century they brough`t with them hundreds of words that eventually found their way into Irish. The Irish language declined temporarily under the Norman warlords but it appears that Irish charm won their descendants over because eventually the descendants of the Normans learned to speak Irish better than English. The indigenous tongue came to dominate once more – but for how long would it last?

IRISH GOES OUT OF BUSINESS

The structure of Irish society was changed forever in the 16th and 17th centuries, when the British Crown consolidated its power in Ireland with a series of **Plantations**. The best lands were given to English and Scottish settlers, who then leased them back to Irish tenants. English became the language of law and business and you needed to speak and understand it in order to gain employment and survive. By the end of the 18th century less than half of the population spoke Irish as their first language. Those who did were the poorest people who had the least to do with the British. Because they were the most vulnerable class, the language was left in a precarious position.

The biggest direct assault on Irish came in 1831 when the ruling British established national schools and prohibited the use of Irish. This initiative was followed by a disaster in the form of the *Great Famine* (1845–1850), which decimated the country's Irish-speaking rural poor. Over a million people died and a tide of emigration began. By the turn of the next century only about one per cent of the population were Irish speakers. Those who emigrated had to learn English in order to survive. On the home front, some political leaders (like *The Liberator*, Daniel O'Connell) and many parents came to think of Irish as backward and a reminder of famine times. They encouraged children to learn English because it was the language of the future. Poor old Irish fell into critical decline and faced extinction.

EMIGRATION & THE DIASPORA

This is one race of people for whom psychoanalysis is of no use whatsoever.
—Sigmund Freud

Millions of Irish people left Irish shores from the 18th century until the twilight of the 20th. Most were poor, uneducated and desperate. Friends and families left behind treated their departures like deaths. The immigrants did what they could to survive, often clustering in groups for solidarity and security. They worked menial jobs, drank too much and crafted a reputation that has plagued the Irish ever since. They were either perceived as coarse and drunken construction labourers who drank and fought too much or *chancers* (dodgy characters) who spoke *blarney* (frivolous nonsense) and were forever steeped in romanticised and deeply sentimental versions of the *Old Country*. These stereotypical Irish characters were referred to by other Irish people using the adjective *Oirish* (which in this pronunciation came to symbolise a clichéd Irishness) and this is how they're still invariably portrayed on stage.

Although perceptions have changed somewhat with the advent of affordable air travel, the Irish themselves cringe at the notion of Ireland that the descendants of the diaspora seem to have: a quaint, mist-shrouded isle of song and story, where hearty old men meet in whitewashed thatched cottages by the sea to play cards, drink *uisce beatha* (literally: the water of life, ie whiskey, pronounced *ish·ke ba·ha*) and recite a tall tale or two. Although, to be sure, there are still a few tiny pockets like this that are invariably cashing in on the tourist dollar.

The proliferation of men called *Paddy* and women called *Sheila* has dogged the Irish ever since. All Irish men came to be referred to as 'Paddies' while, in Australia, where tens of thousands of Irish had been shipped off to the penal colony, all women (not just Irish ones) came to be known as 'Sheilas'. The archetypal Paddy became a much-maligned figure and the butt of a litany of Paddy jokes.

THE GAELIC REVIVAL

The *Gaelic League*, established in 1893, orchestrated a massive push to revive the Irish language and protect its status. This effort was consolidated when the *Irish Free State* was established and it went hell-for-leather into reversing the decline, making the study of Irish a core subject in the school curriculum and setting a minimum standard of Irish as a prerequisite for work in the public service. In 1937, with the birth of the *Irish Constitution*, Irish was declared 'the first official language' of the country (with English as 'the second official language'). But despite officialdom's best intentions it made a *bit of a hames* or *a hash* (mess) of its efforts to keep Irish alive. Instead of making people want to learn it, they tried to ram it down their throats. Many came to resent Irish as a form of penance and rejected it.

HISTORICAL ICONS

Irish people are generally knowledgeable and quite passionate about their history, and most will be familiar with this selection of words and phrases relating to historical events.

To hell or Connaught
When the Irish were being displaced from their fertile, life-giving farms by Oliver Cromwell in the 17th century, he famously advised that anyone who complained could 'go to hell or Connaught'. The province of Connaught was largely infertile so people could hardly distinguish between the two.

Wild Geese
Originally, the *Wild Geese* were the supporters of James II who left Ireland after the Treaty of Limerick in 1691 to form the *Irish Brigade* in Louis XIV's army. The term is also used to refer to all those who left Ireland in the 17th century, and sometimes (loosely) all Irish emigrants.

Flight of earls
This phrase commemorates the events of 1607, when the last leader of Gaelic Ireland, the Earl of Tyrone, Hugh O'Neill, went into exile, taking many Irish lords with him.

St Patrick
The patron saint of Ireland was – shock, horror – actually a Welshman, born with the name Succat. He was kidnapped by Irish raiders and taken to Ireland as a slave, where he herded sheep for over six years before he made good his escape. When he became a priest he took the name Patrick.

The *shamrock* was his prop for preaching the doctrine of the Holy Trinity. It's not known if 17 March is celebrated because it's the date of his birth or of his death. The legend goes that he drove all the snakes out of Ireland, which gave rise to this joke:

Q: What did St Patrick say when he drove the snakes out of Ireland?
A: 'Are youse all right in the back there lads?'

Irish English

Despite all that was hurled against it, Irish refused to go quietly into the museum. Instead it craftily latched itself onto the victor, entwining itself with the dominant language. If English was to be the lingua franca, it would only be so with a strong Irish flavour! Listen to any conversation between Irish people and you'll clearly hear the suppressed melodies and disjunctions of the intriguing grammar of Irish. Regional differences in the dialects of Irish English are basically shaped by proximity to spoken Irish.

For such a small country, there's an astonishing variety of accents, slang expressions, colloquial sayings and divergences in grammar. But although linguistic features differ between regions (most notably between the South and the North) the dialects of Irish English certainly have more similarities than differences when compared to varieties of English spoken in other parts of the world.

The Irish delight in playing with the English language, their manipulations and embellishments giving the language a wonderful range of expressive possibilities. This is perhaps partly why a country not much bigger than Tasmania or the state of Indiana has managed to maintain a massive cultural surplus over the centuries. This fluency is reflected in the works of George Bernard Shaw, JM Synge, Oscar Wilde, William Butler Yeats, Samuel Beckett, James Joyce and more recently Seamus Heaney, Paul Durkan, John Banville, Dermot Bolger, Colm Toibín, Edna O'Brien and many others. It's probably also the reason why the Irish make such good storytellers and comedians and why so many Irish-born people go on to become television presenters and broadcasters.

These successes give the Irish confidence to retain and even build on their linguistic quirks which, in turn, keeps the vernacular alive. But Irish English shouldn't be taken for granted. It has survived in a heavily diluted form from the early 20th century when the establishment actively tried to exclude it from becoming a national language because they deemed it unsophisticated. Even today what remains of Irish English is under threat because schools inevitably try to file the rough edges off the Irish vernacular and attempt to knock it into a standardised shape.

It would be a sad day for the English language if the richness and inventiveness of Irish English were diminished. In the words of US writer TE Kalem, 'The English language brings out the best in the Irish. They court it like a beautiful woman. They make it bray with donkey laughter. They hurl it at the sky like a paint pot full of rainbows, and then make it chant a dirge for man's fate and man's follies that is as mournful as misty spring rain crying over the fallow earth.' Or as the the British theatre critic, Kenneth Tynan, once wrote, 'The English hoard words like misers; the Irish spend them like sailors.'

Irish today

In reality, (as opposed to in the *Irish Constitution* which grants the status of first official language to Irish), Irish survives as a first language only in pockets of Ireland (known as the *Gaeltacht*), largely in remote, rural western and north-western areas which proudly preserve their historical roots. But even here usage is in decline and each national census reveals fewer people speaking it as their first language. It's believed there are now between 20,000 and 30,000 Irish-speaking people living in *Gaeltacht* areas, but another million or so Irish people profess to being able to speak Irish beyond a *cupla focal* (a couple of words).

In an effort to address the state's rather half-hearted attitude towards Irish, the Irish government made the commitment, in 2003, that every publication by a government body would be available in both official languages. However, in what many believe is a sad sign of the times, a report on a new traffic-management system for Dublin published in 2002 revealed that for the first time since the formation of the Irish Free State the vast majority of road signs would be in English only. Even the traditional letter-writing conventions, which begin a letter with *A Chara* (friend) and end with *Is Mise le Meas* (yours respectfully) are in decline.

But it's not all doom and gloom for Irish because, although slowly disappearing as a mother tongue, it's enjoyed something of a revival in the general community in the last 15 years or so. Perhaps as a result of the rapid modernisation of Ireland in recent decades, the Irish don't seem to be as keen on *appearing* modern any more. A new-found cultural confidence is bringing many back to their roots. The number of Irish-medium schools – where everything is taught in Irish – has mushroomed, while the curriculum for Irish in general schools has been stripped of much of its pedantry and made more practical, fun and relevant to the modern world.

As part of this repackaging of Irish, the state has also begun promoting the language through the media, most notably with the launch of *Raidió na Gaeltachta* (Gaeltacht radio) and *Teilifís na Gaeilge* (the Irish-language television station, called initially *TnaG*, now renamed *TG4*). The latter has an award-winning soap opera *as Gaeilge* (in Irish) called *Ros na Rún* (featuring, among other characters, an Irish-speaking gay couple and their child). If you go to Ireland, you should switch on *TG4* to hear the news in Irish every night (with English subtitles) and at least get the flavour of it, although you may need a couple of aspirin afterwards to cope with the incomprehension-induced headache – if you ignore the subtitles, that is.

Seanchai (storytellers)

If you've ever met an Irish man or woman you'll no doubt attest to their fondness for the spoken word. Most seem to have been born with the *gift of the gab*. Through their stories, they're carrying on the great oral tradition of the common Irish people, who preserved (and no doubt embellished) their history through telling stories rather than recording them in writing.

The *seanchai* (storyteller, pronounced *sha·na·kee*) was a very important figure in the community and was awarded great respect. In pre-Christian times, the history – and therefore much of the power – of a clan was entrusted to those with the best memories and a knack for storytelling.

Seanchai have been captivating listeners for millennia, mastering the medium and turning phrases into art. They were important not just for telling tall tales, perpetuating myths and engaging the masses before the dawn of modern entertainment, but also for ingraining in listeners a sense of their heritage and what it means to be Irish. Although *seanchai* still exist, and certainly the spirit lives on today wherever Irish people gather, contemporary storytellers are perhaps more likely to be singers or songwriters.

Ulster English

During the *Plantations of Ulster* in the 16th and 17th centuries, tens of thousands of Scots (and some English) crossed the Irish Sea to settle on Ulster lands given to them by the British Crown. Many of these settlers spoke Scots (which is also called Lallans), a Germanic language closely related to English which was the everyday language of Lowland Scotland at the time.

Their plantations were on such a large scale that these settlers held the balance of economic and political power, and their language gradually took over. Irish had been practically wiped out in the Belfast area by the end of the 17th century. Rural Ulster speech consists of two main dialects, namely *Ulster-Scots*, which is closely related to Scottish English, and the *Central-* or *Mid-Ulster dialect*, which has more influences from Irish. The presence of *Ulster-Scots* (otherwise known as *Ullans*) on the province's landscape has given Ulster a unique cultural pluralism, and it's an officially recognised regional language of Europe.

Although Northern Ireland is a divided society and contact between the Protestant and Catholic communities is limited, there are no clear differences either in accent or grammar between the English spoken by the separate groups. In other words, you can't generally tell which community someone is from by listening to their speech (although the people themselves have tried in the past to differentiate themselves linguistically – see the box 'H for Hostility' on page 204).

Exports

The seeds of Ireland's version of English have been scattered to the four corners of the globe, thanks to the vast Irish diaspora. The influence in places like Britain, the east coast of the US and Australia is obvious, and even the Caribbean, where Irish prisoners were deported, sprouted a bit of 'Irishness'. The island of Montserrat has numerous streets and landmarks with Irish names and you can definitely hear some similarities between the Montserrat and Irish accents.

Thousands of Irish went only as far as Liverpool, just across the Irish Sea and the closest port to Dublin. In fact, so many

---

BOYCOTT OR BE DAMNED

The word 'boycott' meaning 'social excommunication, ostracism or shunning' was unwillingly donated to Irish English by Captain Charles Boycott. Following its adoption by Irish English the word sucessfully spread into other varieties of English around the world. The word has an intriguing history. Captain Boycott was an estate manager in County Mayo in the late 19th century, who in 1880 refused to lower rents or stop evicting tenants despite the fact that they had suffered a poor harvest. The locals adopted a campaign of avoiding all communication and any sort of trade with the captain. Captain Boycott had to resort to importing *Orange* (Loyalist) labourers to run his estate at prohibitive cost and he eventually was forced to pull out and returned to England.

Irish people populated Liverpool over the years that it was often joked that Liverpool was the true capital of Ireland. The Scouse (Liverpool) accent is certainly unlike any other on the British mainland, thanks mainly to the influence of the speech of Dubliners.

Degrees of Irishness

In this section we take a look at the names that have been coined by Irish people to describe themselves and nicknames that have been given to Irish people by others.

black Irish   is a term that is sometimes taken to mean Irish people with dark hair and eyes who, legend has it, descended from the shipwrecked sailors of the Spanish Armada. A variation on this etymology says that they're the descendants of Spanish Moors who came to Ireland for trade. Yet another explanation is that it's common in Irish to give people nicknames based on their hair colour, such as *Seamus dubh* (pronounced *shay·*mus duhv) and *black Irish* is just a carry-over of this into English.

black Protestants   are Protestants who take their religion seriously. One plausible explanation for the name is that in Irish the word *dubh* (black) is commonly used as an intensifier, similar in meaning to 'very'.

bog-trotting Irish or **bog Irish**   is a derogatory name given by imperial forces to the rural and peasant Irish who lived on infertile lands

famine Irish   is the name given to those who emigrated from Ireland (ca.1840–1860) after the devastating potato crop failures at that time

hillbilly was originally used to describe the Ulster Irish settlers in America, mostly Presbyterian, who came in the 18th century and moved southwest into the hills of Appalachia. They looked upon King William of Orange (King Billy) as having given them religious freedom.

lace curtain Irish is a derogatory term for people with pretensions, who tried to give the appearance of prosperity amidst the poverty of shanty life by hanging lace curtains in their windows

plastic Paddy is a disparaging term for someone (often second- or third-generation Irish) who tries to overcompensate for their lack of actual 'Irishness' by living every cliché

real Dublin is an adjective referring to things traditional and usually pretty rough. The term implies authenticity and a connection with a time of poverty and deprivation, and is the antithesis of sophisticated. It can be applied to words, phrases, personalities, accents or anything pertaining to popular culture.

Scotch-Irish are the people of Northern Ireland who are descended from Scottish settlers. The term's commonly used in the United States, but not in Ireland or Scotland.

shanty Irish was used to describe the poorest of the poor Irish immigrants in centuries past; those unfortunate souls who ended up in shanty accommodation

SPEAKING IRISH ENGLISH

For an Irishman, talking is a dance.
—Deborah Love

The Irish certainly have a way with words, particularly the spoken variety, and it's often said they love the sound of their own voices. Fortunately, many others do as well, which encourages them to talk more. But while the **brogue** can be bewitching, and the lilt uplifting, a few Irish accents can also be virtually impossible to follow unless you have a trained ear and the inside track. Generally though, it's quite rightly said that the Irish are among the clearest and most eloquent of English-speakers. But there are also many Irish people that seem to speak a different language altogether, whether it's the lazy, clipped working-class tones of the inner cities or the plummy pretensions of the posh classes.

The pronunciation of Irish English reflects the sounds of the consonants and vowels of Irish, the indigenous language (known as **Gaeilge** in Irish, pronounced *gayl*·ge). Nowhere is

---

THE GIFT OF THE GAB

A talent for flattery is something that the Irish seem to carry in their genes. The origins of this trait reputedly come from Blarney Castle in County Cork and specifically its 17th-century owner Cormac McCarthy, who's said to have talked his way out of many a scrape by misleading the powers that were. Kissing the Stone at Blarney Castle is believed to grant people *the gift of the gab* and has been a popular tourist activity since the 19th century. In order to kiss the Stone, visitors have to be suspended over a 26-metre drop, which naturally becomes a lot higher and a lot more perilous once you've actually been there and are recounting the story.

this more obvious than in the well-known Irish habit of dropping the *h* in words beginning with *th* – when 'thing' becomes 'ting' and 'thirty' becomes 'turty'. The classic tease of foreigners is to get an Irishman to pronounce 'thirty-three and a third' which comes out sounding like 'turty tree and a turd'. You can use this (once only) with ex-pats but don't go trying it with the natives or they might just **trottle ye**.

Pronunciation

Everybody knows and loves the charming, lilting rise and fall of the Irish accent. What is it that actually characterises the Irish accent, though? We'll summarise here a few of the more obvious characteristics.

One of the standout features of Irish English is the heavy emphasis on *r* sounds. The letter *r* is pronounced wherever it is in words – so that the word 'car' is said with a strong *r* sound at the end, for example. Speakers of American English can identify with this, of course, but it's a feature not shared by many other varieties of English. The *r*-heaviness of Irish English means that it's classified by linguists as a rhotic dialect (not erotic, don't get those two mixed up now).

Another feature of Irish English pronunciation is reflected in literary spellings such as **tay** for 'tea' and **paycock** for 'peacock', where the quality of the vowels changes from an *ee* sound to an *ay* sound. Also the vowel sound in the word 'night' takes on an *oy* sound in Irish English, so that it's pronounced like 'noight'. The *u* sound in words such as 'luck' is pronounced more like a double *o*, so that one well-known expletive starting with an *f* rhymes with the word 'book' in other varieties of English.

As mentioned earlier, anyone who has even a passing acquaintance with the Irish variety of English knows that the Irish can't pronounce the *th* sound. To compensate for this deficit perhaps, the Irish are particularly careful to clearly pronounce an *l* wherever it occurs, as in words like 'field' or 'full', where you might just get a long vowel sound in other varieties of English. They also take pains to carefully pronounce the *h* sound in the written combination *wh*, so that the words 'wile' and 'while' sound quite distinct. Another quirk of pronunciation carried over from Irish is the insertion of a neutral vowel (like the *a* in 'ago') between consonants in words such as 'film' (pronounced 'filuhm').

One of the best ways to practise the Irish accent, or train your ear, is to listen to the voices of Irish people in the movies. Try any of the movies below from your local DVD or video rental store. Note that there are some poor impersonators to steer clear of!

- *Angela's Ashes*
- *The Butcher Boy*
- *Circle of Friends* (except Chris O'Donnell)
- *The Commitments*
- *Far and Away* (except for the Americans)
- *The General*
- *In the Name of the Father*
- *Michael Collins* (except Julia Roberts)
- *My Left Foot*
- *The Snapper*
- *The Van*
- *Waking Ned Devine*

IRISH PRONUNCIATION

Many Irish words are incorporated into Irish English and their pronunciation may well be baffling to anyone unfamiliar with the idiosyncrasies of Irish spelling. The name **Siobhán** (pronounced *shiv·awn*) is a well-known illustration. The rules of Irish spelling are summarised on the following page.

Vowels

The letter *a* is pronounced like the short *o* in 'pot'; *e* is short as in 'pet', except when it comes before *a*, when it's silent; *i* is usually pronounced with a long *e* sound as in 'feed'; *o* like the short *u* in 'put'. The acute accent mark (called the **fada**, pronounced fo·da), however, completely changes the pronunciation of vowels, basically making them longer: *á* is pronounced 'aw' as in 'pawn' (or **Siobhán**), *é* like the long *a* in 'pay', and *ó* and *ú*, like the long *o* in 'potent' and the *oo* in 'fooey' respectively.

Consonants

The letter *s* is pronounced 'sh' before *e* or *i*: think of **Sean** (pronounced 'shawn'). The combination *sh*, however, is pronounced 'h', as is *th*. Meanwhile, *bh* and *mh* are pronounced like a *v* or, once in a while, a *w*.

The double-letter combinations *dh*, *fh*, and *gh* are usually completely silent. The name **Laoghaire**, for instance, is pronounced 'leary'. The exception to this rule is the *g* in **Donoghue**, which is pronounced like a breathy *h*. The combination *ch* is the only one that makes some sense in terms of English pronunciation: it sounds like a guttural *k*, as in 'Bach'. The letters *c* and *g* are always hard, as in 'came' and 'game'.

Grammar

YES & NO

There are no words in Irish that directly translate to 'yes' or 'no'. Instead, the verb in a question is repeated in the answer. Quite often the verb is a form of the verb 'to be', so 'yes' is mostly **sea** (pronounced 'shah'), which is literally 'it is'. A negative answer to a question is mostly *ní hea* (pronounced 'nee hah'), which literally translates as 'it is not'. By analogy with Irish grammatical rules, many people – particularly in rural parts of Ireland – have a tendency to use this pattern of avoiding 'yes' or 'no' when speaking English. They usually use the question verb again in their replies – in the positive or negative – in the same tense, voice and person as the question was asked. This is what you might hear:

Q: *Are you finished making the fire?*
A: *I am.*

Q: *Is there petrol in your car?*
A: *There is.*

In Northern Ireland, the Scottish influence is strong and instead of 'yes', they use *aye* (pronounced 'eye'). *Och* (the *ch* is pronounced like the *ch* in 'Bach') is very common as an expression of irritation or frustration and also in the phrase *och aye* 'certainly'. The word *arragh* (dear me, pronounced *a·ra*) is also prevalent, particularly in the North, and tends to be used when something bad has happened and you're being encouraged to get over it and look on the bright side. A phrase like *Arragh, it's broken* implies that it's not the end of the world.

VERBS

Irish verbs have two present tenses, one indicating what's occurring at this instant and another used for habitual or incomplete actions. For example, 'you are now' is *tá tú anois* (literally 'are you now'), but 'you are every day' is *bíonn tú gach lá* (literally 'be you each day'). An example of the use of the habitual tense is the Irish saying *Nuair a bhíonn an cait as baile bíonn na luiche ag rince*. This can be translated into English as 'When the cat's away, the mice dance' which is fine except that the Irish actually uses the habitual present tense form of the verb 'to be' and so a more accurate – to Irish ears – translation is 'When the cat does be away the mice do be dancing.' Rural

Irish English speakers betray this Irish influence and use a ***does be/do be*** construction to discuss habitual actions:

He do(es) be walking home every day.
What does he be doing up there? He be lookin' at cattle.

Another example from Irish English is the frustrated comment of a husband (or lover) who's waiting for his better half to join him for an evening out. The man mutters to himself after looking at his watch ***Jaysus, what does she be at?*** He could have said (for all the good that it would do him) ***What is she at?*** but that would imply that he wanted to know exactly what she was doing at that precise moment in time, whereas the former implies that she's involved in a process (of whose nature he's unaware). The process is not complete (though the person might hope to ***Jaysus*** it was). That's why some linguists call it an 'imperfect' tense … and we're just *beginning* to experience Irish English and its idiosyncrasies.

Irish has no pluperfect tense (a way of talking about one event preceding another) and this is carried over into Irish English. The idiom for 'I had done X when I did Y' is ***I was after doing X when I did Y***, where the word 'after' precedes a verb in the present continous tense (a verb ending in ***-ing***) based on Irish models. The examples below can most commonly be heard used by Dubliners. This feature of Irish English speech is not usually heard in the speech of upper- or middle-class people though. An example:

Why did you hit him? He was after insulting me.

Another peculiarity of Irish English verbal usage is the tacking on of repetitious verbal tags to the end of statements to intensify them. For example, if you saw John and were surprised to see him you might say: *That's John, so it is*. This intensifying device isn't just limited to the verb 'to be', it can also be used with 'to have'. With other verbs, the verb 'to do' is used.

I've finished writing, so I have.
This computer sucks, so it does.

QUESTIONS

It's common to end questions with a *no* or *yeah* in Irish English, to which the exasperated newcomer might finally say, 'Why are you answering your own questions?' It's probably also a defence mechanism against the usually smartarse responses Irish people will give you if you ask a question they deem too obvious. Here are a couple of examples of rhetorical-style questions:

He's not coming today, no?
The shop's closed now, yeah?

ARCHAISMS

Irish English preserves some usages of English that are considered archaic in other varieties of English. One turn of phrase that sounds old-fashioned is the abbreviation of 'it is' to *'tis*, even as a stand-alone sentence. This also allows the double abbreviation *'tisn't*, for 'it's not'. The words *ye*, *youse* or *yis*, archaic in other varieties of English, are still used in place of 'you' plural.

Was it all of ye or just yourself?
What are youse all up to?

Archaisms are not limited to grammatical forms, however. There are a number of words originating in Middle English and Early Modern English which persist in Irish speech but have died out in other varieties of English. The word *bowsey* is sometimes used for 'drunk', **power** is used in the sense 'a great deal of', **disremember** is the quaint equivalent of 'forget' and **wit** is used in the sense of 'mind'.

COLLOQUIAL EXPRESSIONS

Casual conversation in many parts of Ireland includes a variety of colourful turns of phrase. One example is the abbreviation of 'am not' to **amn't** by analogy with 'isn't' and 'aren't'. This can be used as a tag question (*I'm doing it wrong, amn't I?*) or as an alternative to 'I'm not' as in *I amn't joking*. The double negative is also used: *I'm not late, amn't I not?*

Reduplication (repetition of a word) isn't an especially common feature of Irish. Nevertheless, speakers of Irish English occasionally use it in their speech. The Irish *ar bith* corresponds to English 'at all', so the stronger *ar chor ar bith* is the root of the expression *at all, at all*. This expression is however not common in the cities, except when somebody's taking the piss.

Exaggeration and redundancy are common among speakers of Irish English and phrases like *big huge yoke* and *tiny little thingy* are common. *Yer man* (your man) and *yer wan* (your one) are very common when referring to someone you don't know by name but can point out. It's also used in a similar way to the English 'whatshisname'. An example might be *Yer man over there thinks he's God's gift to women*. The response is, incidentally, not *He's not my man!*, though defensive foreigners often say it.

Another common feature of Irish English speech is using the definite article 'the' rather than a possessive pronoun like 'my' or 'your', especially when talking about family members. Look at the following exchange, for example:

Q: *How's the brother?*
A: *He's grand, but the sister has me tormented.*

Also, in informal speech generally the pronoun 'my' is replaced with 'me', eg *Have ye seen me coat?*

The word *now* is often used as an empty word at the end of sentences or phrases, completing an utterance without contributing any apparent meaning, as in the examples below:

Ah, now.	an expression of dismay
Bye/Seeya now.	Goodbye
Hold on now.	Wait a minute
There you go now.	said when giving someone something

(Speakers of some other English dialects also use 'now' in a similar way, but it's a particularly common feature of Irish English.)

The word 'to' attached to an infinitive verb (as in 'to read') is frequently left out where it would be found in other varieties of English. For example, *I am not allowed go out tonight*, instead of 'I am not allowed to go out tonight', is a quite usual turn of phrase in Irish English.

ADJECTIVES

English as used in Ireland relies a lot on intensifying adjectives. Negative adjectives are often turned into positives for this purpose, exhibiting the Irish knack for infusing English with colour:

He shows fierce skill with the ball at centre forward.
He's an awful nice man.

In counties Cavan, Leitrim, Longford, Louth and Meath, a common intensifier is *horrid*:

She's a horrid nice girl.

In Cavan *thunderin'* is another intensifier of choice, particularly in the expression *ya thunderin' eejit*.

Another adjective with the more definite meaning of 'very bad', is **serious**:

He's had a serious run o' bad luck lately.
Ya can run up a serious bill on them mobile phones.

In County Down, they use **brave** to mean both 'many' and 'great' as in **Tha's a brave good motor ya got there**. In Derry, the intensifier of choice is **wild**, as in **It's a wild wet day** but the *d* is often silent so you might hear something like **We had a wile good time**. In Kerry, practically everything good is **powerful**:

He was a powerful footballer.
That's a powerful frock you're wearing.

Used primarily in Wexford, **quern** means 'very', as in **I'm quern tired**.

REPORTED SPEECH

One of the most endearing quirks of Irish English is the habit speakers have of relating news using the present tense and little verbal parentheses like **says I** (from the Irish **arsa mise**) or

---

DOUBLE DUTCH IRISH-STYLE

In most varieties of English you can dismiss someone you don't understand by saying that they're speaking double Dutch. A rough Irish English equivalent is the essentially meaningless expression **Tá sé mahogany gaspipes**, a baffling combination of Irish (the Irish **tá sé**, pronounced taw shay, means 'it is') and English. It's a kind of surreal gag which is meant to phonetically approximate what an Irish speaker sounds like to someone who doesn't speak Irish. The expression originated with the surrealist and satirist writer Flann O'Brien, whose mastery of Irish allowed him to take the mickey out of Irish language fanatics, who were in the ascendant after the Republic came into being.

said he (from the Irish *a duirt se*). For example, when chatting with a neighbour and relaying news of a *row* (argument) with another neighbour, you could hear:

I'm not going to stand for that, says I. And, says he, no-body's asking you to. And I says ... (and so on)

Body language

The appropriate distance to stand apart during conversation in Ireland is about an arm's length. Irish people are as amiable as any race but they might appear slightly aloof at first while they're checking you out. Certainly they wouldn't be expecting any more touching than a handshake. Physical gestures like hugs and kisses for the ladies and manly pats on the back for the men can be worked up to, but don't rush in. Even if you're getting married into an Irish family, you may find the men particularly awkward with showing physical affection. And *for Jaysus' sake*, just because Ireland's in roughly the same neck of the woods as Italy, France and Spain, where men might kiss one another on the cheek and hug, don't think you can get away with that sort of *craic* (sport, pronounced krak) in Ireland – it's an island, and a fairly repressive and uptight one at that!

Of course, if you're a man and you're out with a group of men with *a few gargles on ye* (a few drinks) there's no problem with walking down the street with your arms around each other, professing your mutual and undying love (as long as – and this is of critical importance – neither party owns up to remembering the embrace the next morning).

Swearing

Swearing is quite common and bad language is used freely – at least the Irish version of it, with words like *feck*, *shite* and *eejit* (idiot) which tend to sound more colourful than coarse. Swearwords are even used *midfuckenword* for emphasis. However, we trust you'll always gauge the company before *cussing your mouth off*.

Fecking is a mild swear word, roughly equivalent to 'darned'. It's not a synonym or linguistic watering down of the English word 'fucking' and is not nearly as offensive. The corresponding expletive is *feck*, the noun *fecker*. Many Britons first heard these particularly Irish words in the renowned '90s TV series *Father Ted*, where they were used liberally.

Telling people to *feck off* is common and is mostly said in good humour – it's nowhere near as offensive as telling someone to 'fuck off'. In old Dublin slang, *to feck* is also slang for 'to steal' and a colloquial term meaning 'to throw' as well. If guests overstay their welcome at a party, you might *feck them out*. Mischievous kids might *feck* each other's school-bags over a wall.

Shite isn't nearly as excremental as 'shit' and exclaiming *Jaaysus!* (drawing out the *a* for effect) isn't seen as taking the Lord's name in vain (a mortal sin, don't you know?).

Slang for body parts

The vocabulary of every Irish English speaker is peppered with slang and jargon. It's all right, practically *de rigueur*, to use slang in social settings, but not when doing business. If you want to casually drop some slang words in, you're best advised to stick with the less convoluted slang which will probably be what's recognised and accepted by the main-stream. No other subject matter attracts slang quite as much as parts of the body.

ABOVE THE BELT

Familiar upper body parts and terms to do with the upper body take on new and sometimes surprising forms in Irish slang.

bazzer	a haircut
blue eyes	a nickname for someone who's cross-eyed
Bradleys	underarms, derives from *Brad Pitts* (rhyming slang for 'armpits')
delph	actually means 'crockery' but also used for teeth eg, *a fine set of delph*, or *some delph messing* (ie missing)
flea rake	a comb
gawk	a stare or to stare
guzz-eye	a squint, as in *He has a guzz-eye*
jack russells	muscles – *look at the Jack Russells on yer man*
lugs	ears
mitts	fists
oxters	armpits
ronnie; tash	a moustache (the first term after the movie star Ronald Colman)
scaldy	a bald person
slider; thatch	a wig
smig	a goatee (*smig* is the Irish word for chin)

Irish linguistic creativity has spawned a wealth of synonyms for some other parts of the upper body:

breasts	baps; clackers; dairies; diddies; jabs; knobs; knockers, noddies, punjabs, racks, soothers or tits

face	bake; chevy chase; dial; puss (usually sulky); trap
head or *brains*	loaf; napper; noggin; sally; scone
mouth	cake-hole; gob; kisser; trap
nose	gonker; neb; snout; snoz
stomach	gino genelli; gut; ned kelly

While we're on the subject of heads and the like, sporting flaming red locks is a common physical characteristic of the Irish and reheads are colloquially known as **coppertops**, **copperknobs** or **gingernuts**. **Redser** is a common nickname for a redhead.

BELOW THE BELT

The Irish are certainly not prudish when it comes to coining words for the nether regions. If you're stark naked, you can be described as **bare pelt**, **in the nick** or **in the nip**. This section contains references to physical characteristics and bodily functions too.

bugle; **the mot's crossbar**	an erection
docked	circumcised
gatch	an unusual way of walking, eg *Look at the gatch on him*
hinch	a thigh
hunkers	haunches, eg *There was no seat left so he went down on his hunkers*
jam rags; **brillo pads**	tampons, sanitary towels
pelt	skin
ringed	uncircumcised

Yet again, Irish creativity comes to the fore with a plethora of synonyms for many lower-body parts. A humorous case is that of pubic hair, which is referred to as either **baz** or **fuzz**. **Fuzz**, though, also means 'police'. In a favourite Irish joke a girl is asked if she's ever been picked up by the **fuzz**. 'No,' she says, 'but I've been swung around by the tits a few times!'

backside	arse; behind; derriere; gicker; hole or hoop
female genitalia	box; fanny; flange; gee (with a hard *g*); mary ellen; mary jane or minge
penis	doodle (of children); flute; gooter; knob; langer; large lad; mickey; pecker; pipe; stalk; tool; willy or wire
scrotum; *testicles*	bag; ball bag; bitch; bollocks; flowers and frolics; goolies; knackers; mebbs; sack or yockers

If you hear a woman say that she's *in her flowers* or *having the painters and decorators in* you'll know that she's being coy about menstruating. Quite a different scenario is alluded to in the expressions *there's cheese on your chin, 12 o'clock in China* or *you're flying low*, all of which alert a hapless individual that his fly is open.

Greetings

The head nod is the greeting you're most likely to see in social settings. The nodder is just feeling you out to see if you want to strike up a conversation. If you quickly look away, he'll assume that's because you think he's mistaken you for a friend. The most typical verbal greetings are *Howaya?* or *Howya?* (how are you?). *Hiya* is used by posher people. Some other forms of greeting are:

All roight bud?
How's it goin', sham?
How's it hanging?
How's the body?
How's the form?

Other more elaborate greetings follow:

How are the men? said on entering a non-local pub (usually in the country) when there are a few of the locals present. It helps to break the ice.

How are you keepin'? an enquiry to which you might just hear the reply *Oh, Shakespeare is dead and I'm not feelin' too well myself*

How's it going, head? this is an enquiry as to the welfare of a friend (*head* is a slang word equivalent to 'buddy' or 'mate')

What's da story? (or just plain *Storeeey?*) 'What's up?' or 'What's news?'

Some greetings are regionally specific:

Are you out lookin'at the mornin'? a Kerry greeting

How's about you? usually abbreviated to *Bout ye?* used in Belfast

How's it goin' boy? used in County Cork

How's she cuttin'? used in rural parts generally. A suitable reply is *Grand, altogether* if you're well, or *Survivin'* if not.

Well, boy a Waterford greeting

CHANCING ONE'S ARM

Legend has it that in 1492 a furious argument broke out between two earls in Dublin's St Patrick's Cathedral. When strong words were about to turn to blows, one of the earls barricaded himself into a separate room. The other earl, having counted to 10 and calmed himself down, cut a hole in the door and stuck his arm through, exposing himself to danger while inviting his rival to shake hands. Peace was restored, no limbs were lost, and the phrase *chancing your arm* entered the English language.

Goodbyes

Take note of the turns of phrase below if you wish to bid an Irish person farewell. *God bless* is the farewell of choice for the older generation.

All the best.
Ciao.
God bless.
I'm off.
I'm outta here.
Safe home.

Cheers while this word is obviously a drinking toast, more importantly, it's an all-purpose *aloha*-like tool. You can use it to thank people, to greet them or to say goodbye. Work it in liberally.

Slán pronounced 'slawn'. This comes from a traditional parting exchange in Irish. Literally it means 'health with you'. The person leaving says *slán agat* (pronounced slawn o·guht), and the person staying behind says *slán leat* (pronounced slawn lat). Many non-Irish speakers will just say *slán*.

General chatter

Casually throw in a few of these expressions and you'll blend in nicely with the green green grass of *Éire*.

boy/boyo the start and end of many sentences for Cork people. The latter mostly refers to men that they don't think much of.

c'mere literally, 'come here', but it's really an opener meaning 'come closer/pay attention, I want to tell you something'

em this is the word Irish folk use when pausing to think. It takes the place of the 'um' and 'uh' that other cultures prefer.

Know what I mean? used at the end of a statement and frequently pronounced 'knowwharimean'. The speaker says it for reassurance that they and the listener are on the same page.

lad any man, though usually one of whom you're fond. ***Lads*** plural can refer to men and women in much the same way that 'guys' can.

right? this is another all-purpose expression of determination or clarification (eg *So, that's a gin and tonic for you and a pint for your friend, right?* or *Right, you'll be coming home with me, then?*)

y'know yourself as in 'of course I don't have to tell you this, you already know' or 'I'm sure you'll agree with me on this'

The art of everyday conversation

POOR MOUTH

One of the first things you have to learn about the Irish is that *they're never happy unless they're never happy* (meaning, essentially, that they enjoy a good whinge). The expression *poor mouth* refers to the annoying and congenital custom of always pleading poverty or bad luck. The term comes from the English translation of the novel *An Béal Bocht*, written in Irish by Flann O'Brien. In practice, the penchant for *poor mouth* speech means that it's rare that someone will express unbridled joy for what is. The fear could be that it won't last if other people find out about it. Although generally a gregarious lot, complaints tend to dominate Irish conversations. The rich *pay too much tax* and the poor are *battling just to get ahead*. When things are good they're *bad*, and when they're *bad* they're *desperate altogether*. Here's a short guide to *poor mouth* double-speak:

If you are:	You say:
all right	*Not too bad*
doing a good job	*'Twill have to do*
feeling a bit sorry for yourself	*Not too good*
old	*No spring chicken*
sick	*Got a bad dose; on me last legs*
so-so	*Middling*
well	*Well, considering*

If someone says:	You say:
How's the form?	*I'm on me last legs*
That was very good.	*'Twasn't bad*
Who's there?	*'Tis only me*

EXCESSIVE MODESTY

The Irish don't like to talk themselves up much; in fact, self-deprecation is a much-loved art form in Ireland, and the only thing the Irish like more than belittling themselves is their friends jocularly belittling them. It's generally accepted that the more you talk yourself down, the higher your reality is likely to be. You can never be too humble and your job as a conversationalist is to make your companions feel good about themselves. But all the self-deprecating twaddle also hides a darker secret, and that is that the Irish are, at heart, low on self-esteem. They're therefore usually very suspicious of praise and tend not to believe anything nice that's said about them. Although the Irish wallow in modesty as a sport – and the degree to which they do it is actually a measure of friendship – when you start *slagging them off* (making fun of them), although they'll laugh along, they'll probably fret that many a true word is said in jest.

If you are:	You say:
appreciated	*No bother at all; Not a bother*
complimented on a meal	*'Twas nothing fancy; Just something I threw together*
complimented on your clothing	*Yer pulling me leg; I grabbed the first thing I saw this morning; Are you taking the piss?*
praised	*I did my best*
thanked for something	*'Twas nothing*

CHARM

There is an Irish way of paying compliments as though they were irresistible truths which makes what would otherwise be an impertinence delightful.
—Katherine Tynan Hinkson (Irish poet and novelist)

Both of the habits discussed in the preceding sections are part of this big plan, you see, to be charming. And it's true that nobody does charm quite like the Irish, who it's said could *talk the hind leg off a donkey* and often charm the pants off suitors and tourists! If you want to ingratiate yourself with the locals, trotting out one of these phrases might help:

Type of address:	You say:
acquaintances	*Howya head?; How's head-the-ball?; How's the lads?* (this can include women)
casual	*Howya; Hiya; Hi there*
formal	*my dear man/woman*
friendly	*my good fellow/woman*
informal	*Is it himself/herself?*

Of course, you can't be charming unless you can convince the speaker that he or she is wonderful company and that you've never been regaled with tales quite so astonishing and enchanting before. (The subtext is: don't stop, you're amazing!)

If you wish to convey:	You say:
alarm	*God between us and all harm*
delighted amazement	*You're winding (me) up; Go 'way out o' that!; You're havin' me on!*
enthrallment	*You don't say!; And what happened then?*
relief	*Glory be to God; That's marvellous, altogether*

ACTIVE LISTENING

Even if they're bored, if they want to make an impression, Irish people make sure to appear to be listening intently and are never rude. The table below indicates how to interpret what an Irish listener might say to encourage the speaker.

If you wish to convey:	You say:
agreement	*I know; Too right; Never a truer word said*
a desire to continue the conversation	*Carry on; Go on; Tell me more*
interest	*Is that so?; Jaysus, really?*
praise	*Fair play/fucks/balls to ye!; Isn't that brilliant/marvellous?*

BEGRUDGERY

Perhaps the most famous trait of the Irish – but only recognised by them and generally kept within the wider family – is the affliction of jealousy. As the great Samuel Johnson (the fellow who wrote the first dictionary *ya eejit*) observed in the 18th century,

'The Irish are not in a conspiracy to cheat the world by false representations of the merits of their countrymen. No, Sir, the Irish are a fair people; they never speak well of one another.'

It's a countrywide version of the small-town mentality you find everywhere in the world. It's the kind of burning envy that fuels tribal wars. It's a peculiar disease which seemingly renders the Irish unable to feel good about the successes of their fellow countrymen and women. But, in keeping with the literary thread, we echo the immortal 20th-century Irish writer Brendan Behan, in saying *fuck the begrudgers!*

But even *begrudgery* (known elsewhere, namely Australia, as the 'tall poppy syndrome') has its upsides. In these days of mindless, vacuous celebrity-worship, the Irish reflex of toppling sacred cows on sight can even be quite refreshing.

Name calling

Of our conflicts with others we make rhetoric; of our conflicts with ourselves we make poetry.
—William Butler Yeats

The Irish are generally fairly understanding and will tolerate most social faux pas out of politeness. That said, you should probably avoid discussing politics, history or religion in Northern Ireland at least. If someone asks what religion you are there, the correct answer is *I'm an atheist, thank God* – although this didn't help Spike Milligan. After he was introduced to a crowd in Belfast as an atheist, *an old dear* shouted up, *Is it the Protestant or the Catholic God that you don't believe in?*

If you want to avoid making a *holy show* (spectacle) of yourself in a social setting, then the phrases below could help. The bottom line is: *mind yerself*, *be wide* (be careful) and if necessary *be dog wide* (be extra vigilant), as they say in the North.

FOOLS

If the Irish want to deride someone for being clueless, there's a whole arsenal of expressions available. For example, people can be dismissed as *away with the fairies*, *like a tit in a trance* or, to use some distinctively Irish imagery, *like a lighthouse in the bog* (implying that they're brilliant but useless). To cut someone down to size for an ignorant remark, they might sarcastically say *There's no use in bein' ignorant unless you can show it*. Other ways to describe people who are *not too correct at the top storey* are:

as thick as ...
 an ass
 a brick
 a ditch
 a plank
 two short planks
 a stone
 a wall

as slow as a wet week
as soft as shite
away in the head (Belfast)
he doesn't know his arse from his elbow
he hasn't a titter of wit
her head's a marlie
 (*marlie* is slang for 'marble' – a child's toy)
one wit more and she'd be a half-wit
not the full shilling
there's a want in him

A word that has a wider meaning in Ireland than in standard English is *thick*. In Standard English it means either 'the opposite of thin' or, used judgmentally, 'a simpleton'. In Ireland, it can also mean 'aggressively defensive and stubborn', eg *He got thick when I asked him for the money.*

Idiots also get short shrift by being labelled in a multitude of ways: *balloonhead, bleedener, bullroot, cabbage, caffler,*

Name calling

43

clart, clift, coof, dope, dozer, dunce, eejit, fecky the ninth, gam gimp, gobaloon, gob-daw, gobshite, gom, gomeril, gowl, guipe, mit, mook, moylee (literally a cow with no horns), *mug, muppet, oinseach, plonker, tin-roofer, sap, spa, spacer, spanner, spoofer, tube, welthead, a wreck-the-head* or a *yahoo.*

If someone's engaging in *codology* (foolishness or nonsense) they can be told off for *acting the cannat* or *maggot*, or for their *ballsology* or *blather and twaddle.*

GOODIES & BADDIES

A good reliable salt-of-the-earth type of person is described as *a sound man, a good sort, a good skin* or *a soul of decency.* A villain or troublemaker, on the other hand, is a *bad beast, bad egg, bowsey, git, gouger, gurrier, gutter snipe, hardchaw, header, mentaler, sham-feen* or *tarjar.*

Getting on your wick

TEASING

To tease in Irish English is to *cod, let on* or *slag.* If an Irish person wants to let you know that they're teasing you they might say *I'm only messing with you, I'm only buzzin' wit ya, I'm only pulling your leg, I'm only slagging.* If you're after a handy rebuttal to having the mickey taken out of you, try these expressions: *D'ye think I came down with the last shower?, Do you think I came up the Lagan in a bubble?* (Belfast), *Do you think I was born yesterday?, Do ye think I came up the Liffey in a banana boat?* (Dublin), *Pull the other one, why don't ye!, Me elbow!, Away on!, Away with ye!* (Belfast), *Get lost, Me arse!, Yer ma!*

IRRITATION

If you're in a cranky mood in Ireland you're *brassed off*, *cheesed off*, *browned off*, *as cross as a bag of cats*, *driven up the wall*, *fit to be tied*, *pissed off* or *up to 90*. Someone or something that's annoying you could be described as *getting on your wick/tits* or *doing your head in*. You might be driven to abuse someone: in the local parlance, *eat the head (or face) off someone*, *give someone the length and breadth of your tongue* or *give out*. If you're on the receiving end you might get *a right bollocking*, *a barge* or be *dragged over the coals*.

CONFLICT

If you're being dragged into a *ballyhooly* or a *donnybrook* in Ireland you're in for an argument (also known as a *carry-on*, *ructions* or, playfully, *twistin' hay*). Make sure, though, that you don't *lose your rag/the head*, *go nuts/bonkers*, *take a bluey*, *lose your Paddy*, *throw a Paddy* or *lose the head* (lose your temper) or you could end up in an *aggro*, *scrap*, *mill*, *bull and cow*, *Barney Rubble*, *reef*, *reefin'* or *mangle* (a fight). You might just incite someone to *bat* (in Northern Ireland), *belt*, *clatter*, *clobber*, *clock*, *dig*, *dunt*, *lamp*, *puck*, *skelp* or *tullock* (in County Cork) you – all of which mean 'to punch'. If things get really heated, you might even want to suggest that you and your opponent step outside using one of the following phrases:

Are ye starting?
Do you want your eye dyed?
Do ye want yer teeth in a bag?
D'ye want yer go?
I claim ya!
I'll bleeding burst ya!
I'll brain ye!
I'll do you!
Whatcha lookin' at?

Someone who shies away from a fight might be labelled a *chicken*, *feardie*, *poltroon* or a *scaredy cat*.

More than grand

Grand is a very common term for when everything's great. When you need something stronger and want to talk up something outstanding, there's a vast store of superlatives to draw upon: *bang on, beezer, brill, chiming, class, cracker, deadly, dead on, gallery, gameball, gift, gilt-edge, the job, legend, magic, massa, massive, mega, mighty, philly, powerful, rapid, savage, smashing, stickin' out, top shelf, a weapon, wicked*. All these terms can be emphasised with the prefix *bleedin'*. And when a thing is the genuine article, the real deal or simply the best, you can glorify it with these expressions: *the dog's bollocks, the mutt's nuts, the puppy's privates* or *the cat's miaow*.

Less than

When something's not up to scratch or no good, it's *brutal, cat, desperate, diabolical, mouldy, murder, poxy* and *shite*. If you feel these are still lacking, embellish with *bleedin'*.

A little add-on with a lot of meaning

The suffix *-ín* (anglicised as *-een*) is used extensively in Irish and Irish English, and has a whole host of different connotations. Our favourite is when it's added to the end of words to soften them or convey affection, as when it's added to someone's name or nickname (like the Irish word for 'darling'

SHONEENS

Shoneen is a largely obsolete term for an Irish person who collaborated with the British administration in Ireland – or by extension anyone who adopted British customs. In its most general sense it denotes a traitor.

---

mhuirnín). It's also used to describe smallness (as in *boreen* 'a small lane' or *girleen* 'little girl'). However, it can be disparaging and denote something or somebody sneaky and dishonest (like a *squireen* 'a small and pretentious landowner'). Here are a few more commonly used *-een* words:

colleen	a girl (from Irish *cailín* 'girl')
crusheen	a small jug such as those used for whiskey
drisheen	blood sausage; black pudding
gulpeen	someone who's a bit slow on the uptake
gurteen	a small field
shebeen	an illicit drinking house
sleeveen;	a sly type
slinkeen	
spalpeen	a scamp; an irresponsible fool

Weather

May the wind be always at your back,
the sun shine warm upon your face and
the rain fall soft upon your fields.
—part of an Irish blessing

It's said that there are only a few types of weather in Ireland and you may see them all in one day. Mostly, it's either raining for weeks at a time or the country's enjoying a *dry spell* (a break, all too temporary, from the rain). Ireland is warmed by the Gulf Stream, which flows through the Atlantic Ocean. NASA reckons that without it, it'd be 15°C cooler on average but that's not to say it isn't cold enough already. It's also responsible for the heavy rainfall which defines Ireland in so many ways (the *Emerald Isle* wouldn't have 40 shades of green without it) and the relatively low snowfall.

The Irish are so fond of talking and complaining about the weather that you need to be armed with a few choice adjectives to enter even the most basic of conversations. Most often, you'll hear the prevailing conditions described as **fierce**, **desperate** or **brutal** – whether it's cold, too wet or even too hot! If you say *Lovely day we're having*, the reply as likely as not will be *It'll never last*. A local is likely to remark pessimistically on the first sunny day of the year *I suppose this'll be the summer.*

Temperatures around 10°C are considered mild – anything approaching 20°C and the locals are dropping like flies and either running indoors or dragging the family off to the beach complaining loudly, *It's boilin'/roastin'/scorchin' out*. If it's really, really hot (relatively speaking, of course), the catchcry might be: *The sun's splittin' the trees/stones*. At the opposite end of the thermometer, exceptionally cold weather might meet with the exclamation *It'd freeze the balls off a brass monkey!*

Rain generally 'falls' in other countries, whereas in Ireland it **spits**, **skiffs**, **drizzles**, **pours**, **lashes**, **pelts**, **teems**, **buckets** or **pisses down**. If you're caught out in the rain without an umbrella you might get **soaked to the skin** or **wet to the bone** and if you're unlucky enough to step in a puddle, you'll end up with a **posser** (a wet foot) which is of course made worse by having a **hole in yer sole**!

When there's a thunderstorm around, a rumble of thunder might be greeted by the expressions *God's rearranging the furniture* or *the Lord's bringing home the turf*. The expression *a soft day* refers to a mild and rainy day with that particularly Irish soft drizzle or hazy rain also called *mizzle*, that seems to hang in the air waiting for you to walk into it. A *soft day* generally also requires an overcast yet relatively bright sky. The term is a literal translation of the Irish *lá bog* (pronounced law bug).

If you want to join in the chorus of complaints about the weather, you'd better come to grips with this meteorological vocabulary too:

back end	autumn or early winter eg, *It was very wet in the back end*
baltic	freezing cold
close	humid or generally not cold as in *It's very close*
coulrife	someone who feels the cold
dreagh dag	a fine drizzly day
muggy	humid
perished; **foundered**	very cold
possin' wet	soaking wet, generally after being caught in the rain

Police

I have never known a situation where a policeman couldn't make it worse.
—Brendan Behan (Irish dramatist and author, 1923–1964)

The official name of the Irish police service is the *Garda Siochána* (pronounced gar·da shee·ah·kaw·na), which is Irish for 'guardians of the peace'. An individual policeman is a *garda*, while a policewoman is a *ban garda* (literally 'woman guardian', pronounced ban gar·da). The term is translated as *guard* but people also use *garda*. The plural *gardaí* is pronounced gar·dee.

In Northern Ireland the old name for the police, the *RUC* (*Royal Ulster Constabulary*) has been replaced by the more apolitical and less provocative-sounding *PSNI* (*Police Service of Northern Ireland*).

However, on the streets in the North and South, police are also known as *ball hoppers* (rhyming slang for 'coppers'), *bizzies*, *bluebottles*, *cops*, *feds*, *the law*, *mules*, *peelers*, *pigs*, *the razz, razzers, rozzers, shades* and *5-0s*. Here's some other police-related vocabulary:

barracks	a police station (Northern Ireland)
black mariah; *meat wagon*	a police van (a 'paddy wagon' in the US; see box below)
boned; lifted	to seize or arrest
cop shop; pig sty	a police station
gripper	a bailiff sent by the court to seize goods for unpaid fines, etc
jockey; speedy	a police officer on a motorbike
low-fat bacon	a trainee police officer
mockie	a plain-clothes police officer
two bulb	a squad car

PADDY WAGONS

When wave after wave of Irish people fled poverty, famine, oppression and Ireland in the 19th century, Americans took to calling them all 'Paddy', which in many cases was derogatory. Struggling to find work and settle in, the Irish developed a reputation for hard drinking and raucous behaviour. Naturally, this brought them into conflict with the law and locals got used to seeing poor Irish people hauled off in police patrol vehicles – as a result these came to be known as 'paddy wagons'. Naturally, the Irish have another name for them: *black mariahs*.

I have a total irreverence for anything connected with society except that which makes the roads safer, the beer stronger, the food cheaper, and the old men and old women warmer in the winter and happier in the summer.
—Brendan Behan

Family, friends and sociability are the cornerstones of Irish life – get close to them and you'll soon discover what makes the Irish tick (not 'thick' now, don't get those two confused).

Although still essentially a Catholic country, Ireland has to a large extent freed itself from the shackles of conservative church teachings over the last decade or so. While abortion is still illegal (except in cases where the continuation of a pregnancy would threaten the life of the mother), Ireland voted – only just – to lift the ban on divorce in 1995.

The biggest changes in contemporary Ireland are a result of its thriving economy, which has gone gangbusters since the mid '90s (when it was first dubbed the *Celtic Tiger* after the similarly robust economies that propelled some Asian countries in the '80s). After centuries of struggle and repeated recessions, Ireland has finally hit its straps. The Irish have never had it so good, and people over the age of 30 still can't believe the change in fortune.

Remarkably, reversing an age-old trend, more people moved to Ireland in the late '90s than left. Dublin, in particular, has become a cosmopolitan hub to rival most major European capitals. The country has also become a destination for economic and humanitarian refugees. This sudden influx of foreigners has taken a bit of getting used to for the natives. The Irish never had to contend with foreigners in such numbers before and their ignorance has bred a little racism, but the new ethnic groups are assimilating into Irish society and putting their own imprints onto this unique and dynamic culture. Typically, the even-more-Catholic-than-the-Irish Poles appear to be the most popular *blow-ins* (newcomers).

The Travellers

Ireland's reputation for welcoming tourists is certainly well earned. The Irish don't, however, appear to be as keen on the indigenous group known as *Travellers*, which numbers around 25,000 people and which is denigrated the length and breadth of the country. Stories abound but nobody really knows the origins of Ireland's *Travelling People*, who have a distinct and vibrant culture typically associated with living in caravans and roaming in search of work and away from trouble.

Sometimes mistakenly linked to the Roma people (otherwise referred to as Gypsies), Irish *Travellers* are in fact of Irish origin and have their own distinct language known to academics as *Shelta*. In the 19th century they were most closely associated with tinsmithing, which earned them their now almost quaint alternative name of *Tinkers*. Most of the population today know them derogatorily as *Knackers* or *Cream Crackers*. They associate *Travellers* with crime and ripping off the State, and refuse them entry to many pubs and other amenities. They really are, by and large, treated like second-class citizens and their reputation for trouble is perpetuated by a sometimes sensationalist media.

Irish *Travellers* are predominantly Catholic and have a complex culture which is largely misunderstood and belittled by the hostile majority. An interesting fact – which taken on its own only feeds prejudice – is that Irish *Travellers* have the world's highest incidence of intermarriage between cousins. Individual families are components of much larger wholes, from which they derive meaning and security. Every family member is cherished, and the elderly are revered. Weddings are lavish affairs, bringing together hundreds of relatives to socialise, celebrate and *put down* (arrange) more marriages. Fairs are also huge and popular occasions, and the trading of horses – an activity central to *Traveller* identity in Ireland – is usually a key part of these get-togethers.

Travellers' preferred and traditional way of dealing with conflict – of which they do seem to attract more than their fair share – is to move on, which is perhaps partly why they've never really been able to stand their ground in the face of prejudice. Despite this, several thousand *Travellers* in Ireland are now accommodated on *halting sites*, where they live in mobile homes but have access to basic amenities. More again live in standard local authority housing. Many live around Dublin, although there are some towns that have sizable populations of *Travellers*, most notably Rathkeale in County Limerick and Tuam in County Galway. *Travellers* generally refer to the non-travelling community, even those who live in the cities, as *country people*.

Religion

Among the best traitors Ireland has ever had, Mother Church ranks at the very top, a massive obstacle in the path to equality and freedom. She has been a force for conservatism… to ward off threats to her own security and influence.
—Bernadette Devlin (Irish politician and the youngest member of the British House of Commons, from 1969 to 1974)

Ireland has undergone a social revolution in the last decade or so. Practices once forbidden by the Catholic Church are now permitted. Contraception is freely used and divorce is legal (and Ireland's divorce rate is today on a par with other European nations). Controversially, abortions may be performed if the life of the mother is threatened. (Conservative anti-abortion groups are still trying to get rid of even this concession, despite the fact that some 6000 women go from Ireland to England to have abortions each year, adding the air fare to the emotional toll.)

Although Irish society has challenged the dominance of the Catholic Church, Catholicism remains an important part of Irish customs and culture and, bucking the trend, churches have reported increased attendances, which is perhaps due to a portion of the population feeling like it has to pay penance after the hedonistic materialism that took hold at the turn of the millennium.

A pious person or religious zealot can be described as a **buck nun, crawthumper, holy jo** or a **votcheen** and be dismissed as someone who **hugs the altar rails** or **kisses the statues**. The vocabulary below relates to religious matters. While some of it is not unique to Ireland, you're likely to hear these words and phrases in religious circles:

black Protestant	a devout, staunch Protestant
chapel	a Catholic church (Northern Ireland)
diocese	an area made up of many parishes and under the jurisdiction of a bishop
Father	any priest, just called **Father** if you don't know his name
genuflection	the act of bending the knee and bowing towards the altar before taking your seat in church
good-living man	a very religious man
man of the cloth	a priest
micky dodger	a celibate woman; a nun
novena	a special prayer held over several days to a particular saint or deity
parish	any area that has its own church and clergyman
penguin	a jocular term for a nun
start dinner like a fox	to begin eating without first saying grace

the angelus a minute's silence for prayer. A bell tolls at noon on the radio and 6pm on the television to let anybody who's interested know that it might be a good time for a little prayer. The *angelus* has been religiously transmitted (pardon the pun) by the national broadcaster RTÉ ever since television was introduced.

catechism a manual of Christian doctrine presented in a question-and-answer format, used primarily in schools in preparation for confirmation

Christian Butchers the Christian Brothers – a lay teaching order renowned for the religious emphasis in their teaching and for being strict disciplinarians

the collection the collection of monetary offerings during mass. A box or basket is passed around for the congregation so they can chip in towards the upkeep of the church and priest.

font a small decorative basin usually near the front door of a house or church, which contains *holy water* people dip their fingers into before making the *sign of the cross*. A much larger *font* is used for baptising babies.

holy water water blessed by a priest and used to bless oneself. The higher up in the Church the person who's blessed the water is, the holier and more sought-after it is. Catholics returning from holy pilgrimage sites such as the Vatican, Lourdes or Knock will always bring back *holy water* for themselves and as gifts for friends.

kicks with the other foot; ***one of the other side*** someone of a different religious denomination to the speaker (generally used to refer to either a Protestant or a Catholic)

Magdalene asylums homes for 'fallen women' which were operated extremely strictly by the Catholic Church. An estimated 30,000 women were admitted to these institutions during their 150-year history. The last *asylum* only closed its

Religion

doors in 1996. They attained notoriety in the 2002 Irish film *Magadalene Sisters*.

press-button-bee a jocular term for a Presbyterian. Comes from the old public phone boxes which had a button *A* to press when your call was answered, and a button *B* to get your money back if the call wasn't answered.

sign of the cross the sign made with the right hand, touching the head, chest, left shoulder and right shoulder in turn whilst saying 'in the name of the Father, Son and Holy Spirit'. The ritual can be made fun of by replacing the prayer with the ditty ***spectacles, testicles, wallet and watch*** – this profanity usually committed by Protestants or lapsed Catholics.

souper someone who converted from Catholicism to Protestantism for personal benefit. It comes from the Great Famine in the 1840s, when Protestant churches offered soup to the hungry on condition that they convert (see the box on page 113 in the Food & Drink chapter for more).

vocation the honourable calling to serve the Lord as a priest or nun, or sometimes a lay teacher. The term is often used by members of the education profession when talking to their charges about career options.

DIVINE EXPRESSIONS

A big difference between Irish English and other varieties is the number of expressions that make reference to religion. As already mentioned, Ireland was a profoundly Catholic country until the '70s (it's still Catholic but the all-pervasive influence has waned) and every aspect of its culture has been heavily influenced by Roman Catholicism. You'll often hear the Irish use phrases like ***God bless*** or ***Safe home*** when parting company. This habit is actually even more common in Irish. It's quite usual to hear people saying *the blessings of God upon you*, which is almost a direct translation of the Irish phrases *Beannacht Dé ort* (to one person) and *Beannacht Dé oraibh* (to more than one person). Other examples of references to God include: *God love you*; *with the help of God*; *where in God's name did you get that?* or *for God's sake*. Religion was so much a part of life that God gets mentioned very regularly indeed. In a particularly frustrating situation it's common for the Irish to summon *sweet Jesus, Mary and Joseph* and all the saints as well!

PATRON SAINTS

In Catholicism there's a whole gallery of *patron saints* that can be invoked in your hour of need. You may well hear pious Irish people pleading with some of the following:

St Anthony	can help you find things you've lost
St Brendan	(known as 'the Navigator') he suposedly inspired Christopher Columbus
St Brigid	the patron saint of babies and famous for the tiny crosses which she made from rushes
St Christopher	the patron saint of travelling, popularly depicted on medals carrying the Christ-child across a river on his shoulders
St Francis of Assisi	looks after animals and the environment generally
St Gerard Majella	the patron saint of expectant mothers
St Jude	is the one to turn to for hopeless causes
St Patrick	the patron saint of Ireland

You can also invoke the *the man upstairs* (God) directly using the expressions below:

God love you! (an expression of pity)
God is good! (indicates an optimistic outlook)
The Lord looks sideways on you. (an ill wish)
God never shuts one door but he opens another. (a consoling phrase)
God bless the work! (a greeting to workers)
The light of Heaven to you! (a blessing)

Of course, along with religious piety comes a healthy respect for the devil who's inspired a number of sayings. There are a few curses you can trot out if someone's being *a right divil* or a bit of a *chancer* (someone who stretches the truth or is false).

A pack of cards is the prayer book of Old Nick.
It's hard to dance with the devil on your back.
May you be in heaven an hour before the devil knows you're dead!
That fella's as sharp as the devil's needle.
The devil's curse on you. (strangely, this is actually a blessing)
The devil's own children have the devil's own luck.
The poor old divil. (shows pity for someone who's having a hard time)
When you eat with the devil, use a long spoon.

THE WAKE

Although traditional *wakes* aren't all that common in Ireland any more, elements of the custom remain strong and the Irish certainly know how to put 'fun' into a funeral. It's often joked, in fact, that the only difference between an Irish wedding and an Irish funeral is that there's one less person drunk at the latter.

There's between three to four days from the time a person dies to when they're buried. In that time, dispersed family and friends converge on the family home, sustained by food often prepared by neighbours and whiskey, which is generally the drink of choice for the occasion. It's very rare that the deceased will be laid out for all to see as in the old days but the spirit of the affair is the same; it's not only a celebration of the life just passed but a send-off to the next one. Singing is very likely – someone will start off with a rendition of the deceased's favourite song or songs and it will carry on from there.

The root of the traditional Irish *wake* lies in the special bonds of family and community in Ireland. As they bid farewell to loved ones, whether because of death or emigration, the scene is one of celebration mixed with sadness.

Superstitions & beliefs

If you are lucky enough to be Irish, you're lucky enough.
—Grace Boyle

Every culture has its superstitions but – whether they're a result of suspicion, pessimism, a fondness for the drink or just a predilection for tall tales – Ireland certainly seems to have more than its fair share. Of course, you'll already know that breaking a mirror will bring you seven years of bad luck, but did you know that *If you tell your dreams before breakfast they'll come true*? Or that *Happy is the bride the sun shines on, happy the corpse the rain pours on*?

One of the pervasive supersitions in Ireland is encapsulated in the phrase *A Saturday flit is a short sit*. Traditional wisdom is that if you move house on a Saturday some disaster is sure to follow (there's a chance this tale was concocted by Ireland's first removalists, who reckoned people shifting house and belongings themselves on their one day off might be bad for business). This also applies – in theory – to such things as going into hospital for treatment, coming out after you're cured or even going on holiday. The medical profession in Ireland have researched this and found that a disproportionate number of patients choose to check out on Friday or stay in until Sunday!

There are other Irish superstitions that you might not have heard of, many of which can be traced back to pagan beliefs or early Christianity and survive in some form to this day. We'll examine a few over the following pages.

BLACK CATS

If your path is crossed by a black cat, you've got some good luck heading your way, unless of course you're the first person that the black cat sees in the morning. If that happens you might as well go back to bed because nothing good's going to happen all day.

DEATH

If a wild bird enters your house or a picture falls off the wall, you can expect a death in the family. The clearest indication of the arrival of the Grim Reaper, though, is when you hear the wailing of the *banshee* (see Mythical Creatures, page 62).

DOMESTIC SITUATIONS

A knife falling on the floor means a male visitor is coming. If it's a fork, expect a female. If you drop the whole cutlery drawer you can expect sore toes. Crossed knives on the countertop or table? Better uncross them immediately or there'll be a *row* (argument) in the house.

Itchy palms have a particular significance. If the palm of your right hand is itchy it means you'll soon be shaking hands with a stranger. If the left hand needs a scratch you're about to receive money. (If both palms are itchy you've probably got dermatitis.) And if you're the forgetful type, take note: if you've left something behind in the house, you can't just go back into the house or you'll bring on bad luck. You'd better knock and get somebody to hand it to you.

A DREAM DATE

Girls who put a small piece of wedding cake under their pillow dream of the man they're going to marry. Funnily enough though, to actually dream of a wedding is considered very bad luck indeed.

THE FAIRY BUSH

If a farmer has a bush or tree in the middle of a field, he'd better not cut it down, as the fairies dance around it during the dark hours. It's called the *Fairy Bush*. If he does cut it down all manner of misfortune will befall his family. This superstition is particularly well known in Northern Ireland.

GIFTS

Giving the gift of a cross in any form will bring bad luck to the receiver. Giving a prayer book is as good as saying the friendship is over. Give someone a handbag, purse or wallet and you'd better put some coins in it (the coins are traditionally called a *hansel*). Never give the gift of a knife.

MAGPIES

There's a superstition relating to the sighting of magpies. The saying goes: *one for sorrow, two for joy, three for a girl, four for a boy, five for silver, six for gold, seven for a secret never to be told.*

NEW YEAR

On New Year's Eve it's considered good luck if the first visitor of the New Year is dark-haired. What usually happens is that a suitable visitor already in the house is sent outside just before the clock strikes 12 and knocks to be allowed entry afterward, ensuring good luck for the household in the coming year! Before they open the front door to admit guests to New Year celebrations, many Irish people open the back door – to let the old year out before admitting the new one.

JUST PLAIN BAD *CESS* (LUCK)

The seriously superstitious should note that a pregnant woman mustn't go to a funeral or into a graveyard. No one should ever open an umbrella indoors, put shoes (particularly new ones) on a table or chair, place a bed facing the door, cut their fingernails on a Sunday or drive a green car. If someone has a reputation for being unlucky, others might say *She's that unlucky she wouldn't get a kick in a stampede*.

MYTHICAL CREATURES

A long time ago, new mothers commonly feared that their newborns might be changelings – fairies which take the shape of humans to get ahead. If the proud new parents were suspicious of having a fairy in their midst, the mother would hold the child and cross a river. If the baby was a changeling, rather than a baby, it would reveal itself rather than go near the water. Sure everybody knows fairies can't stand water!

Legend has it that the *Púca* (pronounced poo·ka and also known as *Pooka*, *Phouka*, *Púka*, *Glashtyn* or *Gruagach*) is a nimble shape-changer that can appear as anything from an eagle to a large black goat (the Irish for which is *poc* – this apparently inspired the goat-footed satyr Puck in Shakespeare's *A Midsummer Night's Dream*). However, it most often takes the form of a sleek black horse with a flowing mane and glowing yellow eyes, just in case you spot one when driving around the country.

The mythological creature that most associate with Ireland is, of course, the *leprechaun*. The name comes from the Irish *luprachán* (half-bodied). The *leprechaun* takes the form of a little old man with a cocked hat and leather apron. He jealously guards a hidden pot of gold which he can only be made to part with if he's threatened with physical harm. Those who wish to steal a *leprechaun*'s treasure must keep their eyes on him, for if they look away for even a second, the *leprechaun* will vanish and along with him the promise of treasure. Like other mythological races in the Irish tradition, *leprechauns* are considered to be partly real, physical creatures and partly spirits.

A *banshee* is a female spirit whose anguished, blood-curdling wailing outside a house warns of the impending death of a family member. If you hear a number of *banshees* together, it means somebody close to you is about to die.

EMBLEMS

The *shamrock* (clover leaf) is a popular emblem for sports teams, state organisations and just about any Irish organisation (or tradesperson) abroad. As first recorded in 1726, the clover plant was used by St Patrick to illustrate the doctrine of the Trinity. It's now registered with the World Intellectual Property Organization as a symbol of Ireland, although it has no official status – the official emblem of the Republic is the harp. The word *shamrock* comes from Irish *seamróg*, (pronounced *sham·rohg*) meaning 'young clover'. Although it didn't make it onto the *Tricolour* (Ireland's national flag), the shamrock features on the flag of the island of Montserrat in the Caribbean, where many citizens are of Irish descent.

The harp is found in the seals of the President, *Taoiseach*, *Tánaiste* (see the Irish politics section on page 87 for an explanation of these terms) and government ministers, and is used on the back of new euro coins minted in Ireland. The Presidential Standard is a blue flag with the heraldic harp.

Oh, and anyone who has downed a *Guinness* or two might have noticed that a harp is also the trademark symbol of that iconic Irish drink. The model for the artistic representation of the heraldic harp is the 14th-century harp now preserved in the museum of Trinity College Dublin, popularly known as the *Brian Boru harp*.

Home

Despite the popularity of the pub, the home is the hub of Irish life and where you'll still be overwhelmed by the hospitality and spirit of the people. Cross an Irish threshold and you may be offered the traditional *céad míle fáilte* (pronounced kayd *mee*·luh *fawl*·cha), which is Irish for 'one hundred thousand welcomes'.

Traditionally, life centred around the hearth – replaced in modern times by the kitchen, where friends and family generally hang out so they're not too far from the kettle. Enter any Irish home and you'll soon realise that the old stories about Irish mothers making a fuss were no exaggeration. Here are some Irish English words to describe items in your *gaff* or *pad* (your home).

cooker	a stove
covers	bedclothes
delph	crockery
dishcloth	a tea towel
dishrag	a dishwashing cloth
dresser	a sideboard
hot press	an airing cupboard, where the hot water service is
kip; *tip*	a substandard home (however, *take a kip* means 'to have a nap')

kitchen dresser	a wooden display cabinet for ***delph*** (crockery)
parlour	a room set aside for special functions or visitors (eg the local priest), usually the downstairs front room in a house
pinny	an apron
pipes	radiators (for heating)
press	a cupboard
pruheen; ***pruhoge***	a cabin or small house, from Irish ***prochóg*** (pronounced *pro·*khohg)
scheme	a housing estate, especially a Corporation (local government authority) one
scratcher	a bed, for when you need to get some ***zeds*** (sleep)
shore	an open drain outside the back door of a kitchen (now mostly obsolete)
smoothin'	an older person's word for ironing
snib	the latch on a Yale lock
strainer	a colander
winda; windy	a window

Homes in Ireland don't have 'yards'; they have gardens. A ***yard*** is an enclosed, sometimes paved-over, commercial area. All housing estates have an area called ***the green*** where kids meet and play. It's the social centre of the estate, at least for the young ones, and a hub of activity. It can be as simple as a patch of grass, or a much larger park laid out with football fields and playgrounds.

Family

It wasn't too long ago that it would just be expected that Irish women would stay at home, rear the children and do all the housework, while the men barely ***lifted a finger*** or ***did a tap*** (did anything) around the house (or did pretty much anything for which they weren't getting paid). It was often said that Irish men *couldn't boil an egg between them* or that *they're at least 21 before they realise how many sugars they take in their tea*! Whether it's the loosening of gender strictures or just the astronomical cost of mortgages these days, there's no doubt that Ireland has accelerated rapidly into the 21st century. Now it's common for middle-class women to juggle both career and family, while at long last men are expected to *shift their arses* and help out with the chores.

English words for family members often have a number of colourful Irish English equivalents:

baby	babby; dote; galya; mite; snapper (sometimes preceded by **bread/ankle**); sprog; squealer; tiddler; wain
boy	cub; gasoor; gossoon
brother	one and other; small/young fella
child	childer (Belfast); chiseller; nipper; our fella; wane (North)
daughter	bottle of water
father	auld man; the da; ole fella
girl	blaid; cutty; gahilla (Cavan)
grandmother	granny; nana
mother	the ma; morr (Northern Ireland); ole wan
parents	folks
sister	our wan; skin 'n' blister; young wan
son	currant bun
wife	ball and chain; her indoors; struggle and strife (all borrowed from English slang)

Although the last two words for 'boy' look and sound suspiciously like the French *garçon*, their true origin is the Irish word *gossure* derived from *gos* 'branch' and *úr* 'fresh, new' (literally 'a young shoot').

Given the importance of family life in Irish culture, it's not surprising that there are a good few sayings on the theme:

A family of Irish birth will argue and fight, but let a shout come from without and see them all unite.

An old man's child is hard to rear.

Blood is thicker than water – and easier seen.

Bricks and mortar make a house but the laughter of children makes a home.

No son is as good as his father in his sister's eyes. No father is as good as his son in his mother's eyes.

Praise and scold in equal measure, if your family you treasure.

The family that has no skeleton in a cupboard has buried it instead.

What's bred in the marrow comes out in the bone.

Surnames

As English rule extended across Ireland from the 15th century onwards, and Irish immigrants scattered around the English-speaking world, Irish surnames were commonly anglicised (changed to sound more English). The anglicised Irish names were often transformed by faulty phonetic spellings, with the result that several seemingly different surnames might actually have the same Irish root. For example, the Irish *O'hAodh* (meaning 'fire') covers a number of different family trees and was converted to *Hughes*, *Hayes* and *O'Hay*, amongst others.

It's very common for people of Gaelic origin to have surnames beginning with *O'* or *Mc* (less frequently *Mac* and occasionally shortened to just *Ma* at the beginning of the name). The prefixes *Mc* and *Mac* mean 'son of'. *O'* comes from

Ua (originally *hUa*), which means 'grandson', or 'descendant'. The descendants of Brian Boru, the High King of Ireland, were known as the *O'Brien* clan, for instance. Some common surnames that begin with *O'* are: *O'Neill, O'Brien, O'Leary, O'Donnell, O'Toole, O'Malley* and *O'Hara*. Some names that begin with *Mc* are: *McDonagh, McDonald, McGuinness* and *McGuire*. *Fitz* is an Irish version of the old Norman word *fils* meaning 'son', and features in surnames such as in *Fitzgerald, Fitzsimmons, Fitzgibbons* and *Fitzpatrick*.

Clothing

If you hear an Irish person talking about putting on their *bluchers*, *bodycoat* and *duncher* to go out in the rain, you might well be bamboozled. There's a whole distinctive vocabulary attached to clothing in Ireland, don't you know. Take male underwear, for example, referred to variously as *bags*, *jocks*, *trolleys*, *undercrackers* and *underjocks*. For all the rest, see the list following:

bodycoat	an overcoat (Kilkenny)
bluchers	heavy boots (pronounced 'bloochers')
cacks*; *strides	trousers
drawers*; *knickers	women's underwear
duds	clothes in general
duncher	a cap
gansie*; *jumper	a sweater, pullover or jersey (comes directly from the Irish word *geansaí*)
glad rags	smart clothes

gutties; runners	running shoes
housecoat	a dressing-gown
knicks	sports shorts
lid	a flat cap
new threads	new outfit or item of clothing
rushers; wellies	Wellington boots, gumboots
sancey	a well turned-out guy
shipyards	large shoes
simmet	a vest, singlet
snot rag	a handkerchief
swimming trunks	a man's bathing suit
zoggabongs	springy head adornments *flogged* (sold) by *aul' wans* (middle-aged or elderly women) at Christmas, football matches and St Patrick's Day

The phrase *I've got great wearin' out o' (this coat)* means 'I've had it for years and it still looks great'. If you hear a man referred to as a *dickey dazzler* or a *mickey dazzler*, the implication is that he's overdressed. Being done up in your Sunday best, however, is being *dressed to the nines*.

City dwellers

Urban rivalry is rife in Dublin, which has developed its own lexicon of denigration.

a howya	someone from the suburbs
a jaysus howya	someone from a very outer suburb
cadger; toucher	someone who tries to *touch* or *tap* you for money; a beggar
DNS	acronym for *de north side* – derogatory term for the north side of Dublin and/or its residents
knackeragua	a rough area

chuggers people looking for you to join up or donate to a charity. They stand on street corners looking for passers-by to *touch up*. The warning phrases are *Spare a minute?* or *Can I have a word?* Don't make eye contact and keep walking. Derived from the expression 'charity mugger'.

mickey marbh slang for Stillorgan, a suburb of Dublin. Comes from *mickey* – a childish term for 'penis' (the 'organ' part of the suburb name) and the Irish *marbh* (pronounced mor·uhv) 'dead' (the 'still' part).

silkies working-class or Corporation (local government authority) estate Dubliners who seem to wear nothing but shiny acrylic tracksuits

Outsiders

Dublin was the administrative base of the British government when it controlled Ireland, and even today the rest of the country regards Dubliners as a gang of hoity-toity *jackeens* (named either after their allegiance to the Union Jack or, according to other sources, after 'John Bull', the stereotypical name for an Englishman). Dubliners, for their part, regard the inhabitants of the rest of the country as a mob of uncultured *bog-trotting culchies* (country folk). It's a friendly rivalry for the most part but that doesn't reduce the frequency or the intensity of the abuse. The following terms are used specifically to refer to Dubliners:

jack-in-the-box a dead Dublin man

Dublin 4 or **D4** the postal code of the area on the Dublin Southside that encompasses the affluent suburbs of Donnybrook and Ballsbridge. The headquarters of RTÉ, the state television network, and some prestigious private schools are also located there. Wealthy Southsiders have a plummy vocabulary of their own known as *Dortspeak*, after the way they pronounce the train service that connects their affluent homes, (the *DART*, the acronym for Dublin Area Rapid Transport). They say things like *moby* for 'mobile phone', when things don't go exactly as they'd like it's *such a 'mare*, and after any sort of taxing effort they *sooo need a Heiny* (Heineken).

Inhabitants of the country are referred to variously as *boggers*, *bog trotters*, *bog warriors*, *culchies*, *muckrakes*, *muck savages* or *mulchies*. There are a few other more specific terms, too:

buff   another word for *redneck* (see below), mostly used by *culchies* to describe other *culchies* living further out in the countryside, likely to live on a farm up a mountain somewhere

buffalo   a big ugly *fecker* from up the country somewhere

heifer   an unattractive country woman (the consensus being that she looks like a cow)

redneck   anyone who isn't from Dublin. An old Irish joke goes that the name comes from their parents hitting them on the back of the neck, saying *get up to Dublin and get a job.*

Other outsiders also come in for a bit of abuse:

plastic Paddy   someone of Irish descent who has all the accoutrements of Irishness but ends up being a bit of a cliché

Sassenach   (also spelled *Sasanach*) a derisive term for an English person, or a Protestant. It comes from the Scottish Gaelic for 'Saxon', *Sasunach* or *Sasanach* – which is still used in Scotland.

Education

The Irish owe a good deal of their current prosperity to the wisdom of successive governments who, throughout the latter half of the 20th century, always treated the education of their youth as a priority whatever the recession. This stood the Irish in good stead when foreign multinationals were attracted to Ireland because of its highly skilled and relatively cheap English-speaking workforce.

Children enter school aged four as *low babies*, then move on the next year to *high babies*, before starting *primary school* proper. Individual years are referred to as *1st class*, *2nd class* and so on. After *6th class* they head to a *secondary school*. After three years there, they do the *Junior Certificate* (which used to be called the *Intermediate Certificate* or *Inter* for short). They might then have a *transition year* or head straight to another two years of schooling in preparation for their *Leaving Certificate*. If they're bright enough or have worked hard, they might then get a chance to go on to *third-level* (tertiary) education. All very logical terminology, don't you think? There are two recesses during the school day, one for maybe 10 minutes in the morning and an hour for lunch. Guess what they're called? Of course, *little break* and *big break*. Here's some other school-related vocabulary:

amadán	Irish for 'fool' – a favourite teacher's word
biff	a blow to the palm of the hand with a strap or cane as a punishment (now illegal)
clash	to tell tales (also to *tout*)
cog	to copy someone else's work at school
ecker	homework
gushie; rushie	to throw up sweets or coins and have a crowd of kids run to catch them
mala scoile	Irish for 'school bag' (pronounced *maw*·lah *sku*·llya)
marla	the Irish word for 'plasticine' (pronounced *maw*·la)
master	the general term for a male teacher
mill; scrap	a schoolyard fight
Milly up!	a shout that goes up when a fight breaks out

mollies	female students (usually from a girls' school nearby)
muck-truck	a country school bus
mutton dummies	slippers worn at school, because you couldn't wear rubber boots inside
nits	head lice
pruning	when you get your testicles grabbed and squeezed hard, usually when a few guys are holding you down
rubber	an eraser; a condom
sambos	sandwiches
school	pronounced 'skewelle' in Irish English
Sketch!	an exclamation indicating that someone's watching – handy because it can be said without moving the lips
snared	to be caught doing something against the rules
snared rapid	to be caught red-handed
specky four-eyes	a merciless nickname for anyone who wears glasses
steelers and scrunchers	large marbles used to knock ordinary marbles during a game

canted kicked a football over a wall, eg *You canted the ball, ya eejit*. It implies that you can't get the ball back – on the other side of the wall there's usually a big dog or a mean person.

college more like the American English than the British English usage; it usually refers to any sort of *third-level* (tertiary) education institution, be it a college, university or Institute of Technology

give a deadner   to knee someone in the side of their thigh, or to punch them at the top of their arm, giving them a dead arm or leg

thunder and lightning   comes from 'to knock like thunder and run like lightning': knocking at a door and running away (also called **knick knacking**)

And more odds and sods related to school which have several Irish English equivalents:

pencil sharpener   parer; pencil parer; topper

playing truant from school   bunking off; mitching; on the hop; on the ockie

someone who tells on you   a rat; a snitch; a squealer; a squaler; a clashbeg

There are inevitably more than a few acronyms associated with education in Ireland:

CAO	Central Applications Office – the body that manages the process by which students are awarded places at **third-level** colleges
DCU	Dublin City University
NUI	the National University of Ireland (comprising the University Colleges of Dublin, Cork and Galway – **UCD**, **UCC** and **UCG** respectively – and Maynooth University)
RTC	Regional Technical College – **third-level** colleges situated in various cities and offering certificate, diploma and degree courses
TCD	Trinity College Dublin
UCC	University College Cork
UCD	University College Dublin
UCG	University College Galway
UL or **UoL**	University of Limerick

Work

It's not that the office environment is formal – more that the Irish are inherently over-polite – but it's common to hear managers preface requests to subordinates with *Would you ever (photocopy this for me)?* Or *Would you mind (doing the job we pay you for)?*

If someone asks you *What line are you in?* they're not talking about a queue but asking what you do for a living, to *bring the bacon home* and all. Of course, work for most is just a means to an end and people often have fairly resigned attitudes to earning a crust. *Another day, another euro* is the way it goes.

You don't 'get busy' when you're working in Ireland either. If things aren't exactly quiet you just say *I'm flat out* or *up to me eyes/teeth/the nines*. If it's really hectic you might be *running around like a blue-arsed fly*.

If you've got a particularly difficult task ahead of you, you might say you *have your work cut out for you*. All this might make you feel an aversion to working at all, in which case others would say about you: *If work was a bed, you'd sleep on the floor*. Here are some other broadly work-related words and expressions:

dole	the unemployment benefit
gaffer	the boss
government artist	a euphemism for someone who draws the **dole**
hambone	an incompetent worker
I'd like me job	means 'No, I won't do it' (whatever it is you're asking me do, which is against the rules)
it does me head in	it's difficult, boring or annoying

me head is wrecked	a lament after a bad day at the office
on the box	unemployed – a Northern Ireland expression which comes from the **box number** (counter position) where you signed on
on the brew	to be in receipt of social welfare payments (Northern Ireland)
the Revenue	the **Revenue Commissioners** – Ireland's tax collection body
the scratcher	Dublin slang for a social welfare payment or the **dole**
sick-line	a doctor's certificate declaring you unfit for work
skiver	someone who avoids work
tastie	a neat and tidy worker; someone good at their job
VAT	Value Added Tax, the sales tax levied in both the Republic and Northern Ireland

nixer a job done on the quiet so that no tax has to be paid on the wages. Often done for payment in kind rather than for cash. A bottle of whiskey used to be a common form of remuneration.

PAYE Pay As You Earn – the taxation system where tax is deducted from your pay packet before you receive it

PRSI Pay Related Social Insurance – a further deduction from the pay of employees to cover certain health and unemployment benefits

Technology

Cellular phones are called *mobiles* or *mobies* for short. *Texting* refers to sending a text message via cellular phone. Much disposable income goes on *putting credit* on your *ready-to-go* mobile, but there are more *bill pay* (contract) customers. If you promise to *give someone a buzz* or *a bell*, you'd better call them later on the *dog and bone* (telephone).

If you want your fingers to do the walking you'll be looking for the *Golden Pages* not the 'Yellow Pages'. As far as the Internet is concerned, in speech addresses are normally spelt out as 'double-u, double-u, double-u dot' followed by any of the following: co-dot-u-k, i-e or com.

Money

Centuries of struggle against poverty mean that the Irish have a healthy respect for money. As they say, *The heavier the purse, the lighter the heart.* As everywhere though, there's a mistrust of those who are driven by money as the following expression shows: *He that is of the opinion that money will do everything may well be suspected of doing everything for money.* Popular slang terms for money include: *Barney Dillons, boodle, bread and honey, dosh, moolah, shekels, shillings, snots* and *spondoolics.* There are a few other slang terms to take note of:

euro	knicker lids; quid; squid; yo-yo (*50 knicker* is '50 quid' – ie euros these days)
five euros	a fiver; nunny bunny; skin diver
flat broke	brassock; skint
loose change	odds; shrapnel
plenty	a score, as in *it cost me a score!*
ten euros	tenner

Tight-fisted individuals can be dressed down using the following treasure trove of disapproving sayings:

She's tight as a cod's arse at 40 fathoms.
He's as tight as a nun's knickers.
She'd peel an orange in her pocket.
He'd give you a fag once a week but that was yesterday.
She'd live in your ear and sublet your eardrum.
He'd skin a flea for a halfpenny.
He wouldn't give you the steam off his piss.
If she had the measles she wouldn't give you a spot.
She'd take the pennies from a dead man's eyes.
That one is so mean she puts the butter on the bread with a feather and takes it off again with a razor.

Toilet humour

Be mindful: in Irish, 'men' is *fir* and 'women' is *mná*. The male facilities therefore may have an F and the female an M. Best to check the universal signs carefully before venturing into the *jacks* (toilets). There are a number of ways to euphemistically describe a call of nature or to excuse oneself to pop off to the *Gary Glitter* (shitter, ie toilet). If you're in a real hurry to get there you can say *Me back teeth are floating* or *I need to splash me boots* (I need to go for a pee). Here are some other ways of indicating that you're off to do *a hit and miss* (a piss) or a *Jimmy Riddle* (rhyming slang for a 'piddle'):

going to drain da snake
going to shake hands with the unemployed
planting a big tree
taking a slash

If, on the other hand, you're in a hurry to do a *shite* (shit), you can say *I'm touchin' cloth*. The act itself can be described as *laying a cable*. Here are a few slang words for a poo:

Barry White*; *Brad Pitt	rhyming slang for *shite* and 'shit'
brown trout	a general term
cork	used by children instead of *number two*

If you're unlucky enough to have a dose of the *scutters*, *squitters* or *steel shutters* (diarrhoea) you can politely say *It's falling from me*. And if someone poisons the atmosphere with a *blinder* (a silent fart) you can try and pinpoint the culprit by indignantly inquiring *Who opened their lunchbox?*

Love & dating

I suppose a ride is out of the question? (do you want to have sex?) is probably not the most subtle way to romance someone, but you might hear it said by some cheeky young drunken *wooer* or *bowsey* (a good-for-nothing person). The usual reply to this or any other unwelcome opening line is *Feck off, ya eejit*. Everyday Irish chatter relating to dating and mating might seem a little crass to the outsider, but just bear in mind that the intention is rarely to offend – if you managed to sit through the whole of the film *The Commitments*, you'll be *grand* (all right). The deed itself is referred to as *the bold thing*, *the business*, *the deed*, *the ham shank* or *a ride* and the act is described as *at it*, *corking the bottle*, *to rock 'n' roll*, *to shag* or *shifting*. For everything else, read on…

Allied Irish	a wank (rhyming slang, shortened form of Allied Irish Bank)
aussie kiss	cunnilingus (similar to a French kiss, but given down under)

beor	an attractive woman (pronounced byor)
bird	girl, generally, or girlfriend
bob	a good-looking man – saying that you want to *give someone a few bob* means you'd like to have intimate relations with them
bobfoc	acronym for 'body off *Baywatch*, face off *Crimewatch*', eg *he's a bobfoc*
brasser	a prostitute who charges *but a brass coin* (ie very little) for her services
cock-block	trying to prevent a male friend from scoring
the cut of his jib	his appearance
cuttie	a young girl
doing a line	courting or going out with someone
doxie	a prostitute who plies her trade on the docks
drop the hand	to gain access to someone's nether regions
erection section	slow set at a disco, when you *lurch* with yer *mot* (girlfriend) or your *fella* (boyfriend)
facin'; neckin'	making out
fella	a male person, also used for a boyfriend
fifty	to be stood up on a date, as in the expression *I got a fifty*
flahulach	flamboyant, also very generous or throwing money around
FM	fuckable mother (ie someone you'd like to fuck)
lurching	up-close slow dancing
out on the prowl/raw	looking for sex
parish bull	a young man with many partners
ride	(as a noun) someone with strong potential; (as a verb) the deed itself

| ***ride knots*** | the birds' nests at the back of someone's hair when they've been on their back bonking all night |
| ***scon*** | an amorous encounter (Kilkenny origin) |

Are they good for the goose/the sauce? do they do the deed? Are they loose?

cute be careful with this term: it has nothing to do with looks but means 'clever' in a sly way. ***Don't be/get cute with me*** is a common saying. ***Cute*** used as an adjective before ***whore*** or ***hoor*** (an alternative spelling), means 'a sneaky, conniving person'.

fla*; *flah an attractive person, or as a verb 'to have sexual intercourse with someone' (from Irish ***fleadh*** 'party', pronounced flah)

get your hole/gee or ***get off*** to score, as in ***Did ye get yer hole last night?*** You might also hear it in the non-sexual phrase ***I will in me gee***, which means 'I've absolutely no intention of doing that'.

pull to have some manner of success with the opposite sex, eg ***I pulled last night*** or ***Do you think he'll pull?*** (the word can refer to anything from a snog to the ***beast with two backs***, ie having sex). Also in the phrase ***on the pull*** which means 'actively looking'. In Dublin ***reef*** is sometimes used for the same thing but is more commonly used to indicate getting caught at something, ***getting reefed***.

shifting a general term that varies in meaning between 'first base' and 'all the way', depending on what part of Ireland the speaker comes from

wear a very deep kiss, with full tongue action. Probably comes from the analogy that you're stuck into somebody so much it's like you're wearing them. The phrase ***to wear the head off somebody*** is to give them an extremely long and hard ***wear***.

A rich vocabulary of synonyms applies to the following intimate language:

condom	50p lifesaver; rubber johnny
girlfriend	hen; lack; mot
masturbate	choking the chicken; pulling yer wire; tuning/pulling yer plum – the last three phrases are also used to mean 'doing nothing', eg in response to the question *What ye doing?*
semen	jip; spunk; spaff
to be pregnant	to be expecting; in the family way; knocked up; preggers; puddeners; up the duff; up the flue; up the pole; up the stick

COMPLIMENTS & REJECTIONS

If a male member of the species wants to express his admiration for a member of the opposite sex, there's an armoury of amorous expression he can call on if he wants to go beyond the standard terms *fine thing*, *fine bit of stuff* or *fine piece of skirt*:

She'd make a cat turn backwards.
She has a backside on her like two rabbits tryin' to get out of a sack.
She has an arse on her like a brewer's mare.
She's a fit bird, I tell ya.
You'd stand to look at her.

And if, in someone's estimation, Nature's been sparing with her gifts, the hapless object of derision can be written off as a *bowler* (pronounced to rhyme with 'fowler'), *minger*, *munter* or *wagon*. You can also say that *his/her face'd stop a clock* or that he/she is *mulgly* (half animal, half human). If someone dresses unfashionably you can say they're *a bit Mary Hick*, *dooley-looking* or *dootsie*.

Other uncomplimentary sayings and expressions:

a face that'd turn milk sour

a face like ...
the back of a bus
a bad stretch of road
a bag of spanners
a hen's arse

he/she wasn't around when the good looks were being handed out

so ugly ...
a bear wouldn't hug him/her
the tide wouldn't take him/her out

Irish politics

This section opens something of a can of worms when we're talking about the whole island of Ireland, as you probably already know. For the record, Ireland is divided into:

- The Republic of Ireland, with Dublin as its capital. This state is usually referred as *Ireland* by its people, and sometimes as *Éire* by outsiders, often people from Britain. Technically *Ireland* and *Éire* are the official names of the state while the *Republic of Ireland* is its official description.

- Northern Ireland is unofficially known as the *North of Ireland* and *Ulster* (although Ulster is the name of a province which also includes Donegal, Cavan, and Monaghan in the Republic). Northern Ireland is part of the United Kingdom.

For some unofficial names used to refer to the Republic of Ireland and Northern Ireland, see the Geographical realities section, page 189.

In medieval times a national Irish kingdom had emerged, headed by an *Ard Rí* or High King of the whole of Ireland. The British took control of the whole island in the 15th century and held it until after the *Irish War of Independence* from 1919 to 1921, when the *Anglo-Irish Treaty* granted independence to the 26 counties of the south. This entity was then known as the *Irish Free State* but would later become the *Republic of Ireland*.

Britain retained control over the six counties of Northern Ireland, which by then had a majority of people (mostly Protestants) who wanted to remain part of the United Kingdom. This was largely the result of the *Plantation of Ulster*, with the Crown giving rich agricultural lands to Protestant settlers from Britain from the 17th century on. The desire to remain part of the United Kingdom still exists today and has been the root of the bitter conflicts that have fuelled *the Troubles* throughout recent decades. The conflict has settled considerably in recent years, however, with a renewed and sustained push for peace.

In a number of areas, the island operates officially as a single entity: for example, in most kinds of sports. The major religions – the Roman Catholic Church, the *Church of Ireland* (the Protestant church) and the *Presbyterian Church in Ireland* – are organised on an all-island basis. Some 92 per cent of the population of the Republic of Ireland and over 44 per cent of Northern Ireland is Roman Catholic. Some trade unions are also organised on an all-Ireland basis and associated with the *Irish Congress of Trades Unions* (*ICTU*) in Dublin, while others in Northern Ireland are affiliated with the *Trades Union Congress* (*TUC*) in the United Kingdom – though such unions may organise in both parts of the island as well as in Britain. The island also has a shared culture across the divide in many other areas, such as traditional music.

The island is often referred to as being part of the British Isles. However, many people in Ireland take exception to the suggestion that – God, forbid – both islands belong to Britain. For this reason, the term *Britain and Ireland* is commonly used as a more neutral alternative.

REPUBLIC OF IRELAND POLITICAL TERMS

Set against the backdrop of a divided Ireland and influential religious lobby groups, political life in the Republic of Ireland is often turbulent. This heady atmosphere has given rise to the expression *flying a kite*. When a politician or senior civil servant releases a suggestion into the public domain in order to gauge the reaction, it's often said that he or she is *flying a kite*. Such kites are generally 'flown' when the government attempts to solve a tricky problem in a manner which some may deem controversial. Below are some other words and phrases associated with political life in the Republic of Ireland.

Bunreacht na hÉireann (pronounced *bun·*rakht na *hayr·*in) the Irish Constitution; mainly written by Eamon de Valera in 1937 and amended several times through referendum. Articles II and III have been controversially used to claim the whole island and were therefore disliked by *Unionists*. As part of the peace process, these were removed by referendum in 1999.

chancer not only used in a political context but for anybody who puts on an act, stretches the truth or is false

the Corpo the local city authority

cute whoor in its broadest sense this refers to an Irish person, usually male and from a rural background, whose *gombeen* (see next page) antics have drawn some grudging admiration. Very commonly used by politicians when describing each other.

Fianna Fáil (pronounced *fee·*na fawl) traditionally the largest single party in the Republic of Ireland. Formed by Eamon De Valera at the end of the 1922–23 Civil War; literally translates as 'soldiers of destiny' (from some words in the national anthem). Often abbreviated to *FF*.

Fine Gael (pronounced *finn·nu gayl*) the other big Civil War party and traditional enemy of *Fianna Fáil*. Their political opponents often nickname them **blueshirts** after a short-lived fascist party that existed in Ireland in the 1930s (mostly because they know it gets to them). Often abbreviated to *FG*.

gombeen originally, a rural loan-shark. Nowadays, it has come to mean just about any sort of petty underhand or corrupt activity (or the mindset possessed by those engaged in such activities) practised by people from the country, eg *pulling strokes* (confidence trickery) or *fiddling* EU subsidies.

Irish Free State the original name given to the 26 counties that were granted independence from Britain and went on to form the Republic of Ireland

PDs the Progressive Democrats – a fiscally conservative centre-right party that formed as a breakaway from *Fianna Fáil* and is now its most likely coalition partner

rubber-chicken circuit the endless series of public dinners and luncheons politicians must attend to raise funds and make speeches. The food often includes chicken which is cooked hours earlier and then reheated, giving it a rubbery texture. Refers especially to social functions organised by the *Fianna Fail* party in the '70s and '80s.

GENERAL GOVERNMENT TERMINOLOGY

Below are some key terms describing Irish political organs and offices:

Ceann Comhairle	(pronounced *kyown kaw·*la) speaker (also known as the chairman) of the *Dáil* (Parliament)
Dáil	(pronounced *dawl*) the lower house of the Republic of Ireland Parliament
FEC	Fair Employment Commission – a body which judges cases of religious discrimination in Northern Ireland

IDA	Industrial Development Authority – a Republic of Ireland agency which tries to attract foreign investment
IDB	Industrial Development Board – the Northern Ireland equivalent of the *IDA*
Leinster House	the building where the *Dáil* and *Seanad* sit
Oireachtas	(pronounced *ir*·akh·tis) the name covering both houses of the Irish Parliament (ie the *Dáil* and the *Seanad*) and the President
Seanad	(pronounced *sha*·nid) the upper house of the Republic of Ireland Parliament
Secretary	a government minister of State, usually the one responsible for Northern Ireland

Tánaiste	(pronounced *taw*·nash·ta) the deputy Prime Minister of the Republic of Ireland
Taoiseach	(pronounced *tee*·shock) the Prime Minister of the Republic of Ireland
TD	Teachta Dála (pronounced *chok*·ta *daw*·la) a *Dáil* Deputy or a Member of Parliament in the Republic of Ireland
Uachtarán	(pronounced *ookh*·ta·rawn) the Irish word for 'president'
Westminster	shorthand for the British parliament and/or government

SEMI-STATE BODIES

The term *semi-state body* refers to a company in which the Irish government has a controlling stake. Here are the main *semi-state bodies* in the Republic of Ireland:

Aer Lingus	the state-owned airline
An Bord Bia	(pronounced an bord *bee*·a) the Food Board – responsible for the marketing of Irish food products (except fish) overseas
An Post	the postal service in the Republic of Ireland
BIM	Bord Iascaigh Mhara (pronounced bord *ees*·kee *wa*·ra) the state body with the responsibility for promoting the fishing industry
Bord Gáis	the Gas Board
Bord Fáilte	(pronounced bord *fawl*·cha) the Irish Tourist Board – literally 'welcome board'
Bord na Móna	(pronounced bord na *moh*·na) the state-sponsored body responsible for peat production
Bord Tráchtala	(pronounced bord trakh·*taw*·la) the state board to assist Irish exporters
Coillte	(pronounced *kwill*·cha) the Irish Forestry Board
DART	Dublin Area Rapid Transport – the suburban rail service which operates between Howth and Greystones
ESB	the Electricity Supply Board
TÉ	Telecom Éireann (pronounced *tel*·a·kom *ayr*·in) – Ireland's telecommunications company
TG4	the Irish-language television service

VHI Voluntary Health Insurance – the largest semi-state health insurance company in the Republic of Ireland

CIÉ Coras Iompar Éireann (pronounced *ko·ras um·per ayr·in*) – the Republic of Ireland bus and rail transport company, which comprises **Iarnrod Éireann** (Irish Rail, pronounced *eern·rod ayr·in*), **Bus Átha Cliath** (Dublin Bus, pronounced *bus aw·ha klee·ya*) and **Bus Éireann** (Irish Bus, pronounced *bus ayr·in*)

RTÉ Raidio Teilifís Éireann (pronounced *rad·ee·oh tel·a·feesh ayr·in*) – the Irish state broadcasting company often accused of harbouring **Dublin 4** attitudes. **RTÉ1, TG4** (the Irish-language television channel) and **Network 2** are its two television channels.

IRISH POLITICAL HOUSEHOLD NAMES

Gerry Adams
Leader of *Sinn Féin*. Although he is regarded by many as a long-time apologist for the *IRA* – even a former leader – Adams has been instrumental in the Northern Ireland peace process and in bringing the *IRA* to the negotiating table, which led to their official disbandment in 2005.

Bertie Ahern
The salt-of-the-earth, straight-talking, pint-drinking, football-watching Dubliner who has been *Taoiseach* since 1997.

Brian Boru
High King of Ireland credited with driving the Viking invaders out of Ireland in the Battle of Clontarf in 1056 and leaving the Irish free to spend over a hundred years fighting amongst themselves before the next horde of invaders arrived.

Edward Carson
Barrister and leader of the *Irish Unionist Party* until 1921, Carson proposed the exclusion of Ulster from Home Rule and supported the *Ulster Volunteer Force* in 1913.

Michael Collins
After cutting his teeth as a *Republican* leader in the Easter Rising, Collins became head of intelligence during the *War of Independence* against the British and was renowned as a ruthless and skilled strategist. He was accused by many *Republicans* of being a traitor when he was sent to London – against his wishes – to negotiate the terms of a treaty. Collins led the pro-treaty faction in the ensuing Civil War and was shot dead by anti-treaty forces in Cork in 1922. He was denigrated during the long political reign of De Valera (his old comrade turned Civil War adversary), although his status as a great Irish leader has since been restored.

Charles J Haughey
Veteran *Fianna Fáil* politician and renowned scoundrel, Haughey was *Taoiseach* many times during the '80s and was brought before a long list of tribunals on charges of *graft* (political corruption).

King Billy

The nickname for William of Orange, the Dutch Protestant who wrested the British throne from the Catholic tyrant James II (who had made his last stand in Ireland).

Daniel O'Connell

Popularly known as *The Liberator*. An Irish political leader and MP at Westminster in the early 19th century, O'Connell campaigned long and hard against anti-Catholic laws and to repeal the Act of Union to Britain. He is remembered as the founder of a nonviolent form of Irish nationalism. O'Connell is thought by many to be the greatest leader of his time.

Ian Paisley

Fiery churchman and head of the *Democratic Unionist Party* (DUP), Paisley was at the time of writing the most popular and intransigent *Unionist* in Northern Ireland (and the most despised by *Republicans*). He's closely associated with the famous catch-cries 'No surrender' and 'Ulster says no' (generally to any negotiations with *Nationalists*). He's getting on a bit but is likely to be succeeded by his equally hardcore son, Ian.

Charles Stewart Parnell

A late-19th-century politician and first President of the Land League and later an MP and leader of the Home Rule Party. He was an effective parliamentarian known by many as the 'uncrowned king of Ireland'. His demise followed his scandalous affair with Kitty O'Shea; he died after her divorce and their marriage in 1891.

Eamon de Valera

The only commander not to be executed after the 1916 Easter Rising armed rebellion against British rule (because he'd been born in the US), De Valera emerged as victor in the Irish Civil War and went on to become the most important 20th century Irish *Nationalist* politician. He was the founder of *Fianna Fáil* and President of the Executive Council and *Taoiseach* during the periods 1932–48, 1951–54 and 1957–59. He was president of the Republic of Ireland from 1959–73 and died in 1975.

NORTHERN IRELAND POLITICAL TERMS

Of course, political life in Northern Ireland is a veritable ferment of controversy and conflict. The terminology below conveys the bitter schisms at the heart of Northern Irish life:

the Cause refers to the primary aim of the *Republican* movement – the restoration of a united Ireland

chuckies supporters of the (provisional) *IRA* and *Sinn Féin*. From *tiocfaidh ár lá* (pronounced *chu·key awr law*), a Republican slogan meaning 'our day will come'.

DUP Democratic Unionist Party – Ian Paisley's party; usually tries to be more radical and intransigent than the *UUP*

Fenian rebel a derogatory term aimed at Catholics, especially those thought to sympathise with the *IRA*. The term comes from the name of a mythical tribe that were totally self-reliant and apparently loved Ireland so much they couldn't be fussed ruling the world.

free state bastard/free stater a derogatory term for a citizen of the Republic of Ireland, used by Northern Ireland Protestants and those Catholics who believe people south of the border sold them out

hood a term of endearment used by *Loyalists* for their paramilitaries

hun a derogatory term for a Protestant and/or *Unionist*, as they're loyal to the Windsors, who were originally German

IRA Irish Republican Army – the main *Republican* terrorist group – officially disbanded in 2005. Also known as the *Provisionals* or the *Provos* or referred to fondly by *Republicans* as *the boys*, *the lads* or *the ra*.

jaffa an Irish Protestant (named after the *Orange Order* via Jaffa oranges)

Loyalist someone who wants to preserve the cultural and political links between Great Britain and Northern Ireland

and who's willing to use force in the fight to preserve these links. A *Unionist* is less keen on the violence. Both are mainly Protestant.

marching season during the summer months in Northern Ireland, members of the *Unionist* community celebrate their culture by marching with pipe bands and banners commemorating *Loyalist* victories of days gone by. Their routes invariably go through areas populated by *Nationalists* who resent the triumphalism of these marches which leads to annual strife.

mope stands for Most Oppressed People Ever – a derogatory term in Northern Irish political discourse, most often used by *Unionists* when referring to *Nationalists* or *Republicans*. It describes those who claim that no one has ever been as badly treated as they are.

Nationalist synonymous with *Republican* (ie having the aim of linking Northern Ireland to the rest of the island) but more likely to choose political means to this end

Orange Order a *Unionist*, Protestant sectarian organisation in Northern Ireland, named after King William of Orange, the Protestant king who defeated the Catholic King James II at the Battle of the Boyne. The clichéd *Orangeman* – the vicious incorrigible anti-Catholic bigot attired in a sash and bowler hat and defending his right to march where he's not wanted – is a common bogeyman in *Republican* propaganda.

pape; *papish*; *papist* derogatory terms for a Roman Catholic

prod; *proddy* derogatory terms for a Protestant

Republican someone who believes in a united Ireland and is prepared to use force to achieve it. (*Nationalists*, by contrast, prefer political means.) *Republicans* are mostly Catholic.

securocrats *Unionists* and British government officials who *Nationalists* believe place disproportionate emphasis on security issues as a way of excluding them from government

RUC Royal Ulster Constabulary – the Northern Ireland police, now called the *Police Service of Northern Ireland* (PSNI)

SDLP Social Democratic and Labour Party – traditionally the main Catholic and *Nationalist* party

Sinn Féin a party with close ties to the *IRA* that gets most of its support in Northern Ireland (but has increasing numbers of supporters also in the south). Literally translated as 'we ourselves' and pronounced shin fayn.

slasher a large *Lambeg* drum (Irish traditional drum) used by *Orange* bands in their marches

Stormont the old parliament building in Northern Ireland – often used to refer to the parliament itself

taig a derogatory term for a Catholic (from *Tadhg*, Irish for 'Timothy', pronounced taig)

the twelfth (of July) the highlight of the *Unionist marching season*, it celebrates the victory of the Protestant English King William of Orange over the Catholic King James II, at the Battle of the Boyne in 1690

Unionist a supporter of union between Britain and Northern Ireland

UUP Ulster Unionist Party – traditionally the main *Unionist* party in Northern Ireland, it has lost popularity in recent years because of its support for the peace process; sometimes known as the 'official' *Unionists*

PARAMILITARY GROUPS

The bloody war of attrition between *Republican* sympathisers determined to end the British presence on the one hand, and *Loyalists* determined to preserve British rule over Northern Ireland on the other, has spawned a host of paramilitary groups employing brutal tactics. Here's some of the vocabulary associated with these groups:

An Phoblacht/Republican News the official newspaper of the *Irish Republican Movement*, known by both its Irish name (pronounced on *fub·lokht*) and its English name

Continuity IRA a splinter group opposed to the peace process

INLA Irish National Liberation Army – another *Republican* terrorist group

knee-capping the best-known punishment carried out by paramilitaries – shooting victims through the knee cap

LVF Loyalist Volunteer Force – an extremist *Loyalist* terror group

ÓnhÉ the Irish Volunteers (stands for *Óglaigh na hÉireann*) – a term often used by Republicans to refer to the *IRA* but lately used by *RIRA* (the *Real IRA*) to refer to themselves

punishment beatings when paramilitaries take the law into their hands and punish people in their own communities for 'anti-social behaviour'

Real IRA a splinter group that disagreed with the *IRA*'s ceasefire and 'constitutionalism'. It's also known by the acronym *RIRA.*

Red Hand Commandos a *Loyalist* terror group; often said to be a cover name for the *UVF*

UDA Ulster Defence Association – an umbrella group for various *Loyalist* paramilitary and terror groups

UVF Ulster Volunteer Force – a *Loyalist* terror group

UFF Ulster Freedom Fighters – another *Loyalist* terror group; also a cover name for the *UDA* as a whole

Current affairs

REPUBLIC OF IRELAND

The words and phrases below either mark seminal events in the political life of the Republic of Ireland or are words or phrases that might be used in connection with current affairs.

Brendan Smyth Affair   the case of a paedophile priest and the delay in his extradition from the Republic of Ireland to Northern Ireland that led to the defeat of the *Fianna Fáil/* Labour coalition government in 1994

CAP   Common Agricultural Policy – the EU system of farm subsidies which make up the largest portion of EU spending. This system has, according to one school of thought, allowed Irish farmers to remain on the land and rural communities to thrive. According to others it's a wasteful and expensive system which has allowed Irish agricultural producers to grow food for which there is no market but still get paid a good price.

graft   means 'hard work' in some countries but in Ireland these days it means corruption in government, as allegedly perfected by former *Taoiseach* Charles Haughey. He served for seven years from the late '80s and allegedly received millions in 'gifts' from prominent businesspeople at a time when the country was struggling economically. The scandal gave rise to a series of seemingly interminable tribunals, which implicated a host of other politicians and created a new millionaire class of barrister because they went on for so long and cost the State so much money.

GUBU   an acronym coined by a well-known journalist after Charles Haughey (*Taoiseach* at the time) described the discovery of a killer in the flat of the Attorney General as 'grotesque, unbelievable, bizarre and unprecedented'. Came to be used as tongue-in-cheek popular shorthand for all scandals involving him.

Indo the *Irish Independent* – the daily newspaper with the largest circulation in Ireland

the Irish Times Ireland's broadsheet newspaper

X Case the infamous abortion rights case that ensued when a teenage girl who had been raped by an adult friend of the family was physically prevented from travelling to England to have an abortion. The case resulted in a referendum in 1992 to 'clear up' the issue which resulted in the Irish people saying no to abortion in such cases.

NORTHERN IRELAND

Here are a couple of seminal events in Northern Ireland political life:

Downing St. Declaration a joint Anglo-Irish communiqué issued in November 1995 which started the policy of parallel 'tracks' of negotiation – one for arms decommissioning and one for all-party talks

GFA Good Friday Agreement – the Northern Ireland settlement to end the *Troubles* negotiated up until the early morning of 10 April 1998, supported by majorities in NI and the Republic of Ireland in two simultaneous referenda in May. Also referred to variously as the ***Belfast Agreement***; the ***Stormont Agreement*** and the ***British-Irish Agreement.***

Irish America

Around 34 million Americans claim Irish ancestry – more than any other ancestry except for German. Many of these Irish Americans still identify with their ancestral home. Catholic Irish Americans actively supported Irish independence. Even today, elements of both Catholic and Protestant Irish-American communities identify with – and even support – their partisan counterparts in the *Troubles* in Northern Ireland.

AOH stands for the Ancient Order of Hibernians – an Irish-American Catholic support organisation founded to assist Irish Catholic immigrants. It coordinates the St Patrick's Day parade in New York.

Clann na nGael was a US-based Irish *Republican* organisation during the late 19th and early 20th centuries. Its aim was to secure an independent Ireland and it was prepared to enter into allegiances with countries against the English to further this aim.

INAC Irish Northern Aid Committee – a US-based *Republican* support organisation. Essentially a fundraising body founded after the start of the *Troubles* in the 1960s. Accused by some of being a front for the *IRA.*

Morrison Visa a US visa named after the Irish-American senator who was instrumental in the scheme that gave Irish people seeking residency in the USA favourable treatment during the late '80s

The most important thing to remember is that time and distance are highly elastic quantities in Ireland. Where you want to go, for example, could be a *long* five-minute walk or a *short* 10-minute walk, depending on your apparent urgency and level of fitness. It might also be a *good* five-minute walk, although never a 'bad' one. If you ask 'How much further?' an Irish person might, to keep your spirits from flagging, take a mile or two off the distance. And you should also remember if somebody says *A mile and a bit* that the *bit* is probably close to another mile. It's no wonder every journey in Ireland takes longer than you thought it would.

Distance

Whether you're nosing around *your neck of the woods* (your neighbourhood) in Ireland or venturing off in search of *Ballygobackwards* (any rural place *down the country*, ie anywhere outside Dublin that the city folk won't have heard of), the phrases below might come in handy.

a fair whack	quite a long distance
hal	over there – supposedly from the Irish *thall*, eg *hal in Galway* (over there in Galway)
miles away	very far
near hand	close by
a stone's throw	close by
strike off	to go or leave, as in *Shall we strike off?*
west	to go back (*Let's head west now*)
within an ass's roar	not far
yonder	over there

abroad outside (archaic English); *I wouldn't go abroad on a day like that – ye'd catch your death o' cowlt*

beyant can mean 'over there', ie in the next field or *townland* (division of land). It can also be heard in the phrase *beyant in the States* (meaning 'in America').

Time

Irish people might use some of these time expressions if they're planning a trip:

again	at some unspecified time in the future, as in the phrase *We'll get ya again* (we'll pay you back next time)
ages ago	long ago
amarach	(pronounced *a·mawr·okh*) Irish for 'tomorrow' and commonly used
bells	o'clock, as in *ten bells* for 'ten o'clock'
a bit	as in the phrase *It's twenty to nine an' a bit*, ie 'it's between twenty and a quarter to nine'
the day	today
the marra	tomorrow
the other day	usually yesterday but can be any day in the previous week
sparrow's fart	first thing in the morning; before dawn (also used to mean 'very small', and to describe anything insignificant)
tamall	(pronounced *to·mol*) a while – *He's been up in Dublin for a tamall now*
whileen; **a wee while**	a while – *wee* is very common in the North

Driving

Within the cities and towns the best and easiest way to get around is *shank's mare* (walking). There's so much to see and so many little side streets (many pedestrian-only) that a car is hardly worth the trouble, especially when parking is at a premium. A single yellow line at the side of the road means no parking at all during work hours; two yellow lines means no parking *at all, at all* (to use an Irish turn of phrase). By the way, there are no 'parking lots' either. There are *parking spaces* or *car parks* (most often parking garages).

Outside the major towns and cities it's really necessary to have a car to get around. As most Irish country roads are narrow, people don't generally go *barrelling*, *booting along*, *ninety to the dozen*, *moving like the clappers* or *tearing along* (driving fast). They save that kind of caper for a *dualler* (a dual carriageway). They're best off *going aisy* (slowing down, pronounced *ay*-zee), particularly if they're driving a *banger*, *crock*, *heap a' shite* or a *jalopy* (a car that's seen better days).

There's no such thing as windshields, only *windscreens*. The *boot* is the trunk and the hood is called a *bonnet*. Oh, and tires are *tyres* and gas is *petrol* (gas stations are *petrol stations*). If you ask where the nearest gas station is you might get a puzzled look or directions to the nearest place that sells natural gas for heating! Here are some other distinctively Irish words to do with cars and driving:

apache	a joyrider
artic	an articulated truck
beamer	a BMW
bogey; gig guider	a homemade go-cart
boreen	the Irish word for a small country road but usually used in English too
car up yer arse	tailgating car
Cool your jets!	Don't lose your cool!
doing a ton	driving at 100mph

doing the rat race	driving through housing estates to avoid the traffic
grease monkey	a car mechanic
hi ace	a van – a small van is called a *transit*
jam jar	a car
jeep	any 4WD/SUV
lorry; lurry	a truck
motor	a car
nifty 50	a 50cc motorbike
put you right	show you the way

lockards guys in peaked caps who appear when you're at tempting to reverse into a parking spot and request you to *Lock 'ard mister, lock 'ard*. They tend to turn up at major events and offer to *mind your car* (to prevent it from being *nicked* or broken into). They each have pitches they *look after* and you're advised to give them a few bob or they might *nick* it themselves.

luck money traditionally, when you bought something second-hand, the previous owner would give you back a token amount of money as good luck. At country fairs sellers still give a euro or two in *luck money* to the buyer of an animal to ensure good luck. The tradition is sometimes still observed with the private sale of motor cars.

monback the assistant to the driver of a lorry (usually a *Guinness* lorry). The word originates from directions to help drivers reverse; *C'mon back, c'mon back.*

muppet mobile; scanger banger hotted-up cars – also known as *boy racers*. Men sometimes spend serious *moolah* (money) doing their cars up.

scutting a dangerous children's pastime, involving hanging onto the back of moving vehicle and *scutting a ride*. It could be as slow as the coal man's horse and cart or as fast as a laundry van.

skimming in Belfast some car owners remove all labels, stickers and official decals on a car – so that no one can tell what make the car originally was!

Public transport & taxis

Sometimes Ireland's mistaken for the northern province of Outer Mongolia because the public transport is so bad. It's getting better, particularly in Dublin with the Dublin Area Rapid Train system (*DART*), and the newer *Luás* tram service. Elsewhere you'd want to pack spare patience.

City buses cover wide areas, run frequently between 7am and 11pm, and bus stops are numerous. In Dublin, there's even a late-night service called *Nite Link* which runs from the city centre to the suburbs. If you're heading in to the city centre, buses have City Centre or *An Lár* (Irish for 'city') on the front.

If public transport isn't your speed you can always catch a *Jo Maxi* (taxi or cab), which you can telephone or hail on the street. Fares are reasonable and taxi drivers are very helpful and good guides for the most part, and don't try to take advantage of you and your lack of knowledge of the area (well, occasionally they might on a trip from the airport).

Holidaying

With more and more money in their pockets, the Irish increasingly take off to sunnier climes for their summer holidays. The most common destinations are the popular beach resorts of Greece and Spain (which are often overrun by Irish people) but choices these days are only limited by imagination and funds. The refrain is *Where are you off to on your holliers?* ('holidays' – also in the expression *school holliers*).

If you ever hear someone talking about getting *the boat to Holyhead*, they're catching the ferry to the town of Holyhead in Wales. In the past, more often than not, this was shorthand for heading over to London in search of work. England is referred to as *across the water* (ie the Irish Sea) while the US is affectionately dubbed *across the pond* (ie across the Atlantic).

Christmas is far and away the biggest holiday in Ireland. In fact, when you want to describe something as really, really big you might say it's *as big as Christmas*. The three weeks leading up to the big day are particularly busy: socialising

PUBLIC HOLIDAYS

The big holidays in Ireland are Christmas (when virtually everything closes down) and Easter. St Patrick's Day is getting bigger by the year and there are a series of public holiday Mondays scattered throughout the year. Everything closes on these Mondays, even the banks, and the three-day breaks they afford are traditionally known as *bank holiday weekends*.

New Year's Day	1 January
St Patrick's Day	17 March
Easter	Good Friday, Easter Saturday, Easter Sunday and Easter Monday (March/April)
May Holiday	1 May
June Holiday	first Monday in June
August Holiday	first Monday in August
October Holiday	last Monday in October
Christmas Day	25 December
St Stephen's Day	26 December

cranks up a gear and lots of emigrants return home to see their families and friends. It can be *murder* (very difficult) trying to get a taxi from town, any town, around Christmas time.

The raucous partying usually comes to a crashing halt for *midnight Mass* on Christmas Eve, after which it's lock-down and you're expected to spend at least a couple of days indoors with family, eating and drinking too much, watching *The Great Escape* for the umpteenth time on *telly* and getting more cranky by the minute. Quality time, don't you know? The day after Christmas Day is called *St Stephen's Day*, not Boxing Day.

As far as Christmas trimmings go, it's usually a candle in the window and a holly wreath on the front door, However, in recent times some locals have also taken to decorating every inch of their homes and gardens, US-style. Oh, and when children pester their parents about what they're getting for Christmas, the standard reply is:

A doll, a drum, a kick in the bum, a chase around the table.

'Irish food is great – until it's cooked,' laughed generations of cynics. Fittingly, in a country laden with so many contrasts and contradictions, Ireland is blessed with an abundance of glorious produce and blighted with a reputation for woeful cuisine. The word *Éire* (Irish for 'Ireland') actually comes from the Latin *hierne*, meaning 'fat and plentiful'. There has never been a shortage of good ingredients; it was just what to do with them that baffled generations of Irish mothers.

But Ireland's bad culinary name was banished (mostly) in the twilight of the 20th century, and now *ating* and drinking is about a lot more than mere sustenance. Nowhere is the new-found confidence of the Irish more evident than at the dinner table. It's a movement you might hear referred to as *New Irish Cuisine*, although the truth is there's not all that much new about it. Ireland's culinary renaissance is merely a self-assured return to a tradition based on simple cooking techniques and the best possible ingredients. Most of the Irish have now been taught not to boil the *bejaysus* out of every vegetable and char every cut of meat.

Drinking, on the other hand, has been in no need of a revival, as you're no doubt already aware. It's the reason that many people travel to Ireland in the first place – the fact that there's decent *grub* may well be considered something of a bonus. Indeed, after you've been infected by the *craic* (fun, pronounced krak) and the humour of a few Irish pubs you might start thinking, like generations of Irish people before you, that food is merely for soaking up the *booze*. Before you get started, get one thing clear: *drink* in Ireland is alcohol; everything else is merely a *beverage*.

In this chapter, we'll give you a taste of the new and poke a little fun at the old, partly because you'll probably still find plenty of it and partly out of *devilment* (mischief).

Eating

Meal times and courses in Ireland present a mini-menu in themselves. *Brekkie* (breakfast) is traditionally a fairly big meal in Ireland. *Elevenses* is a cup of tea and a *biscuit* (a cookie) to tide you over until lunch, while *afternoon tea* is a culinary pit stop on the way to the evening meal, and traditionally – for those who had the means – was quite elaborate and featured pastries and sandwiches. The main meal is known as *tea*, *supper* or *dinner* – the first two being the more rural and traditional names. At the start of your evening meal you might have a light course known as a *starter*; dessert is, helpfully, known as *afters*. When your stomach starts grumbling, these colourful expressions – prefaced with 'I'm so hungry …' – wconvey the need for a feed:

I'm so hungry …
   I could eat a dog's bollocks through a tennis racket.
   I could eat a nun's arse through a convent gate.
   I could eat the lamb o' Jaysus through the rungs of a chair.
   I'd eat a farmer's arse through a blackthorn bush.
   I'd eat the balls off a skunk.
   I'm as weak as a salmon in a sandpit.
   that me belly thinks me throat's been cut.
   the stomach is falling out of me with the hunger after it.

There's more than one way, too, to marvel at someone's appetite if they *put back a huge feed*. You can say that they've *done away with the plate an' all*, or that they've *a wild grá for the food* or bottle (*grá* is the Irish word for 'love' – pronounced graw).

TYPICAL IRISH FOODS

Ireland has a wealth of good ingredients from the land, the seas, lakes and rivers, the wild, the hearth, the farm, the orchard and the fields. And all you knew about was *Irish stew*, eh?

Fish & seafood

Remarkably, for a small island blessed with an abundance of inland and coastal fish the Irish don't really appreciate their good fortune. Almost three-quarters of the fish caught in Irish waters is exported. This anomaly is partly due to the Church decrees that good Christians should eat fish on Fridays and fast days – it subsequently came to be regarded by the Irish as penance food and inferior to meat. Much of what you will find is still often enveloped in batter and deep-fried. It's often said, with good reason, that the Irish live with their backs to the sea. That said, you should sample as much of the local fish and seafood as you can manage. 'Cockles and mussels, alive, alive oh!' was the catchcry of Dublin's famous Molly Malone but it's the west of Ireland that's probably most famous for its shellfish these days, particularly oysters. One terminological difference to be aware of: *Dublin Bay prawns* aren't what you'd call prawns at all, they're lobsters (called 'langoustine' elsewhere).

The salmon has a special place in Irish mythology as the legendary warrior Fionn Mac Cumhaill acquired the gift of eternal wisdom after eating the Salmon of Knowledge. As well as being regarded as brain food, the salmon is associated with health and is part of one of Ireland's original toasts and blessings – *Sláinte an bradáin chugat!* (the health of the salmon to you). Smoked wild Irish salmon is a real treat.

Meat

Even a fleeting visit will reveal how much the Irish love their meat, and it's virtually always the centrepiece of each dish, with everything else mere dressing. *Meat-and-two-veg* is still the standard main meal. In the north they say *meat-and-three-veg* but southerners take the inclusion of *spuds* (potatoes) for granted.

The Irish tend to speak a different language when it comes to meat, and you're likely to hear new terms. A **sirloin steak**, for example, is equivalent to an English rump steak. The cut you might know as a sirloin is a **striploin**. A **hand of pork** comes from the pig's shoulder joint and a **fillet** from the leg. A rack of lamb, known in Britain as the 'best end', is only the **fair end** in Ireland; two racks make a **crown**.

Dairy produce

The Irish word for 'cow' is **bó**, the word for 'road' is **bother** (cow-track) and the word for 'boy' is **buachaill** (cow-boy), these words pronounced 'bow' (like the decoration), bow·her and boo·kil respectively. When you consider that these are pretty basic words in any language, you get some idea of just how important the humble cow is in Ireland. The country's dairy produce is wonderful, and you should savour the butter, milk, cream and cheeses and consider them ample compensation for all that rain (which makes the countryside so green and the cows so healthy).

Vegetables & fruit

As well as the usually trustworthy tuber potatoes, the Irish are fond of a range of vegetables sometimes maligned in other cuisines. Cabbage, when paired with bacon, is one of the best-known Irish side dishes and kale is the king of cabbages. Turnips turn up in winter menus (although we reckon they should be fed to the pigs) and parsnips are also popular. Seaweed, believe it or not, is something of a delicacy on the west and north coasts, particularly a type called **dulse**. Ireland has a proud tradition of apple growing and if you're shopping for apples, bear in mind that they come in two varieties **eating** and **cooking**. Come Friday you'll see mothers filling bagfuls of **cookers** ahead of the Sunday baking spree.

Despite all the talk about a namby pamby **New Irish Cuisine** the **spud** still reigns supreme in Ireland. You can estimate its status by the often regal names the Irish have for their favourite varieties: **Kerr's Pinks**, **Records**, **King Edwards** and **Golden Wonders**. You can call potatoes in general whatever you like –

murphies, poppies, praities, purdies, shpuds, spuds, tatties or *totties*. Here are a few other terms you need to know:

boiled potatoes   are, well, boiled potatoes. But you see, they're boiled because they're too good to mash or whatever else you do to dress them up.

boxty   is a traditional and neglected Irish potato cake fried on a griddle using a mixture of raw and mashed potatoes and eggs. *Linnenhall boxty* also uses garlic to pep it up.

champ   is an Irish dish of mashed potatoes and *scallions* (spring onions)

chips   French fries, which accompany most meals in pubs and small restaurants, particularly outside the cities. In a *chipper* (fish-and-chip shop) you'll ask for a small or large *single* (a single serve of chips).

crisps   potato chips. Sometimes pronounced 'crips' by the locals. *Tayto* (a brand name) *cheese-and-onion crisps* are an iconic Irish snack food.

mash   mashed potatoes, which when accompanied by various additional ingredients become specialities like *colcannon* (see the recipe on the following page)

new potatoes   are, well – this could start getting silly – new or 'new season' potatoes. If you're in Ireland in the springtime you'll notice signs all over the place advertising *New Potatoes*, people talking excitedly about the new spuds and cursing the last season. All that's missing are fanfares and dancing girls. *New potatoes* are usually cooked and served *in their jackets* (with the skins left on) or *skinned* (peeled) on a side plate.

PORCINE PHRASES

While pigs have negative connotations in most countries, in Ireland they're associated with things positive. To say someone *is on the pig's back* is to acknowledge their good fortune. To be *as happy as a pig in shite* is to be, well, pretty happy.

CLASSIC IRISH RECIPES

Colcannon

900g potatoes
450g kale, green cabbage or white cabbage
  (in that order of preference)
200ml milk or cream
2 small leeks, chopped
4 tablespoons of melted butter
salt and pepper to taste

Method

Cook the cabbage and spuds in separate pans of boiling water for about 10 and 15 minutes respectively. Drain cabbage and chop. Drain potatoes and mash. Put the milk or cream in a small saucepan with the leeks and simmer until soft. Mix all together with butter and serve.

The name is from the Irish *cal ceann fhionn* (white-headed cabbage). *Colcannon* is traditionally eaten in Northern Ireland at Halloween. Until quite recently this was a fast day, when no meat was eaten.

Colcannon should ideally be made with chopped kale or green cabbage, but it's also made with white cabbage.

Boxty (potato griddle cakes)

250g raw potato
250g mashed potato
250g plain flour
milk
1 egg
salt and pepper to taste

Method

Grate raw potatoes and mix with the cooked mashed potato. Add salt, pepper and flour. Beat egg and add to mixture with just enough milk to make a batter that will drop from a spoon. Drop by tablespoonfuls onto a hot griddle or frying pan. Cook over a moderate heat for 3 to 4 minutes on each side. Serve with a tart apple sauce, or as part of an *Ulster fry* (with fried bacon, bread, sausages, eggs and black pudding).

Irish stew

450g lean mutton pieces
450g carrots (optional, even controversial, among foodies, who take such things far too seriously)
450g onions
450g potatoes
salt and pepper to taste
pinch of thyme

Method

Place the mutton and thyme in a pot and add cold water to cover. Bring to the boil slowly and simmer for one hour. Add peeled and roughly chopped onions, potatoes, carrots and thyme. Season to taste. Continue cooking until vegetables are tender. Adjust seasoning.

Steak & Guinness pie

1kg round steak
1 tablespoon flour seasoned with salt and pepper
80g lard
8 slices bacon, chopped
5 medium onions
1 tablespoon raisins
1 teaspoon brown sugar
300ml Guinness
chopped parsley
1 recipe of pie crust dough for a double-crust pie

Method

Cut the steak into bite-sized cubes, roll in seasoned flour, and brown in the lard with the bacon. Place the meat in a casserole dish, peel and chop the onions, and fry until golden before adding them to the meat. Add the raisins and brown sugar, pour in the Guinness, cover tightly and simmer over a low heat or in a moderate oven (160–180°C) for 2½ hours. Stir occasionally and add a little more Guinness or water if the rich brown gravy gets too thick. Meanwhile, line a deep pie dish with half the pie crust, and bake it at 180°C for 8 to 10 minutes. Remove from the oven and add the beef mixture. Cover with the top layer of pie crust, and bake until golden.

A SHORT GLOSSARY OF IRISH FOOD

The Irish refer to food in general as *grub*, *nosh*, *scran* or *tucker*. The most popular dishes and ingredients are served up below:

a bag o' bocks an'a swimmer	a serve of fish and chips (County Tipperary)
bangers	pork or beef sausages, almost always fried – the food Irish meat-eaters miss most when they're abroad
bap	a bread bun
cheese	look out for local varieties like **Ardrahan, Blue Rathgore, Cashel Blue, Doolin, Durrus, Gubbeen, Milleens, Orla** and **St Killian**
fadge	a fried potato bread from Northern Ireland
Gaelic steaks	fried beef steaks with a shot of whiskey added to the juices
heel	the undesireable end crusts of a *sliced pan* (the modern shop-bought loaf of bread)
minerals	any carbonated soft drink
MiWadi	the biggest selling brand of cordial in Ireland since 1927
pasty bap	a burger bun containing a burger cooked in batter
potato cakes	leftover spuds usually mashed, shaped into burgers and fried
sambos	sandwiches
scallions	spring onions

Abrakebabra an Irish fast-food chain so called because even though you know the food is disgusting, somehow – as if by magic – you tend to end up there after a heavy *session* in the pub

barm brack a fruit loaf synonymous with Halloween, when it's usually filled with charms wrapped in greaseproof paper. The charms are: a plain gold ring, a sixpence, a thimble and/or a button. Finding the ring means marriage within the year for the person who finds it, the sixpence means wealth, the thimble spinsterhood and the button bachelorhood.

black pudding is a traditional Irish food that's made a come-back in recent years. It's usually made from pig's blood, pork skin and seasonings and the best and most famous version is from Clonakilty, the Cork town it's also named after. ***White pudding*** is a version without the blood. Both are popular.

bubble and squeak is actually an English dish that's found some favour in Ireland. It's basically leftovers fried in a pan, usually in the form of mashed potato patties containing vegetables and perhaps a bit of meat.

coddle (also known as ***Dublin coddle)*** is one of the capital's most famous dishes, although it was never exported – for reasons we can understand. Traditionally served to the ***man of the house*** after he's returned from his Saturday evening ***gargle*** (drinking session), it's a hearty combination of sausages, bacon rashers, onions, potatoes and black pepper in a rich gravy.

colcannon a dish made from mashed potatoes and kale (or cabbage), leeks, cream or milk and butter. Traditionally eaten at Halloween in Northern Ireland with charms inserted into it (see also ***barm brack***).

Connemara lamb a seasonal delicacy, fed on the grass and heathers of the Connemara region of Galway. ***Mountain lamb*** is next best and usually hails from the equally salubrious surrounds of County Kerry.

crubeens an Irish finger food composed of salted pigs' feet or trotters, boiled or eaten with cabbage

THE SOUP TAKERS

During the Irish famine in the late 1840s, many landlords set up soup kitchens to help feed their impoverished tenants. However, some unsavoury Protestant landlords would only give their Roman Catholic tenants soup on condition that they converted to Protestantism. Consequently, people who changed their religion during this time were dubbed ***soup takers***. The phrase is still used to imply somebody who has sold out their beliefs for personal gain.

doorstep a sandwich made with thickly cut bread, often partnered with a cup of tea – as in the expression *a mug of tea and a doorstep*

drisheen is the small intestine of a sheep stuffed with congealed sheep's and cow's blood, oatmeal, milk or cream and seasoning. In Cork it's often paired with tripe.

farl an Ulster term generally used to refer to flat varieties of *soda bread*, potato bread or cakes (potato *farls* or *tatty farls*). A *farl* is a flat piece of bread about 2cm thick with a rough quarter-circle shape.

Fig Rolls are biscuits filled with fig paste that were launched by Ireland's best known biscuit maker, Jacobs, more than a century ago. James Joyce referred to them in his novel *Ulysses*. Hugely successful advertising campaigns tried to solve the puzzle which has perplexed generations of Irish biscuit fans: *How do they get the figs into the Fig Rolls?*

gurr cake a dense fruitcake traditionally made with baker's leftovers, which was popular with street urchins, consequently known as *gurriers*

Irish fry a collection of pretty much anything that can be fried, this is the traditional Irish breakfast from the days when farmers needed something hearty to fuel them for the day ahead. These days, the *Irish fry* is a weekend luxury, best accompanied by the Sunday newspapers and a hangover. You'll need some eggs, bacon rashers, sausages, *white* and *black pudding*, mushrooms and tomatoes. Add a *wee* bit of fried bread and you have yourself an *Ulster Fry*. Add anything else fried and you might have yourself a heart attack!

Irish stew a farmhouse speciality traditionally integral to the Irish diet and symbolic of wholesome survival. The composition of this one-pot wonder has been the subject of passionate debate between purists. Most say it was originally made with mutton, which was the only meat available year-round. Others, particularly in the North, prefer pork spare ribs in their *Irish stew*. Beef can also be used and some historians say that kid was the original meat (see also the boxed text opposite).

mountain lamb see *Connemara lamb*

one-and-one often pronounced 'wan an' wan', a *one-and-one* is the standard order in a *chipper* (fish-and-chip shop) – that is, a portion of fish and a portion (a *single*) of chips. This term supposedly arose because when *chippers* first appeared in Ireland they were run by Italian immigrants who didn't speak much English – customer and proprietor had to resort to sign language: 'one of them and one of them'.

shepherd's pie the perfectly balanced Irish meal, featuring succulent minced beef in gravy topped with a creamy, crispy mash and baked in the oven. Despite the name, this dish is always made with beef in Ireland.

skirts & kidneys is a dish unique to Cork. The *skirts* are trimmings from pork steaks and the kidneys traditionally pork. They're simmered together with onions and usually served with mashed potato.

slider (also known as a *wafer*) a slice of ice cream sandwiched between two flat wafers – not so common in the cities any more, as it's been superseded by the *choc '99* or just *'99* (a soft-serve cone spiked with a Flake chocolate bar). A plain ice cream is a *poke.*

IRISH STEW & THE JOYCE OF COOKING

As humble and as basic as the *Irish Stew* is, it's never been short of admirers. In *Larousse* (probably the most famous food book ever, *ya eejit*), Courtine described it as 'witness, if not of the art of living, at least of the art of staying alive in difficult times.' Ireland's most famous literary son, James Joyce, wrote this in his novel *Finnegan's Wake*:

The more carrots you chop, the more turnips you slit, the more murphies you peel, the more onions you cry over, the more bull-beef you butch, the more mutton you crackerhack, the more potherbs you pound, the fiercer the fire and the longer your spoon and the harder you gruel with more grease to your elbow, the merrier fumes your new Irish stew.

soda bread is the most famous, most Irish and most delicious baked product you're likely to come across. It's made without yeast (because Irish flour is so soft) and is a simple combination of flour, buttermilk and ***bread soda*** (bicarbonate of soda), traditionally baked on the hearth. It's not difficult to make, although Irish cooks concede you must have ***the knack***. It's also known as ***bully bread*** in Northern Ireland, where it's an essential part of the traditional ***Ulster fry***. A sweetened version is often made with the addition of sugar and sultanas, and tastes better than its name – ***spotted dick*** – would suggest.

Drinks & drinking

Actually, I'm a drinker with writing problems.
—Brendan Behan (Irish playwright)

As we said earlier, when people refer to ***drinks*** and ***drinking*** in Ireland it's all about alcohol – the rest are merely ***beverages*** and more appropriately lumped with food. Now that we've got that straight, you should also know that drinking in Ireland is much more than a social activity; it's the foundation upon which Irish culture is built and the reason that, despite a history laced with poverty and oppression, the Irish have always maintained a reputation for good humour and for finding the funny side of things. Take note of the following phrases if you wish to join in the merriment:

I'm dying for a drink.
I'm gummin' for a drink.
I'm parched.
I've an awful throat on me. (not to be confused with ***I've got a bit of a throat on me*** which means I've got a sore throat)
I've a shockin' drooth on me.
Me throat's as dry as Gandhi's flip-flops.
My tongue is hanging out for a jar.

In the unlikely circumstance that you need to talk an Irish person into joining you for a drink at a pub, you can try these phrases:

Are ye on for a pint?
Fancy a few scoops?
What would ye say to a pint?
Will ye go for a jar?

And if things are going well you might be asked *Will ye go again?* (have a second drink). A good response is *Did a bird ever fly on one wing?* If you're thinking of tearing yourself away from the pub, one of your drinking mates might entreat you to *hold your hour* (linger a little longer).

SAYINGS & TOASTS

The favourite national pastime has become enshrined in numerous alcohol-imbued sayings:

An Irish youth proves his manhood by getting stuck into a pint, a woman, and a fish – in that order.

A man takes a drink; the drink takes a drink; the drink takes the man.

Before you call for one for the road be sure you know the road.

The devil invented Scotch whiskey to make the Irish poor.

Drink is the curse of the land. It makes you fight with your neighbour. It makes you shoot at your landlord – and it makes you miss him.

It's the first drop that destroys you; there's no harm at all in the last.

May you have prettier legs than your own under the table before the new spuds are up. (a toast specifically to a bachelor)

Morning is the time to pity the sober. The way they're feeling then is the best they're going to feel all day.

A narrow neck keeps the bottle from being emptied in one swig.

Practice makes perfect, there's many do think, but a man's not too perfect when he's practiced at drink.

Thirst is a shameless disease so here's to a shameful cure.

The truth comes out when the spirit goes in.

WHAT'S YOUR TIPPLE?

Of all Ireland's drinks, the **black stuff** (stout or **porter** as it was originally known) is the most celebrated. While **Guinness** is undoubtedly the most famous brand overseas and the most popular in Ireland, it's only one of three well-known stouts. **Guinness** is brewed in Dublin but gets fierce competition from its southern rivals **Murphys** and **Beamish**, which both hail from Cork and are most popular in the south of the country.

In conversation, particularly between gents using pub toilets (the Irish do like a chat), you might hear another man say he's here with, or had better get back to, the **tall blonde in the black dress**. He'll be talking about his pint of stout! Speaking of pubs, they are of course a big part of the Irish way of life and we tell you everything you need to know about the Irish and their peculiar pub ways in the Pub Etiquette section of the Entertainment chapter.

Another popular pub **scoop** (drink) is **Smithwicks**, a delicious dark ale brewed in the oldest working brewery in Kilkenny, dating from the Middle Ages. You may have encountered a stronger, drier version known as **Kilkenny Irish Beer** which has been widely exported in recent years. It's similar to **Beamish Red Ale**, brewed in Cork. **Caffrey's Irish Ale** is another one to look out for, but traditional **Harp** is best avoided.

Cider has also had a rich history in Ireland ever since the Normans tried to turn the abundance of Irish apples into profit in the 17th century. **Bulmers** is the best known brand. It has made several varieties in Tipperary since 1936 and many Irish people lost their alcoholic chastity to flagons of the stuff out **knacker drinking** – (alfresco drinking, usually by under-age drinkers, student or the lower classes) under bridges, out

in fields, far away from watchful parents and close enough to a shop to buy some mints. Ah … memories.

Spirits are known as **shorts** and local varieties include **Brian Boru Irish vodka** and **Cork Dry Gin**. If you say no to the offer of a beer because you're full or already have a **clatter** (a lot) in front of you, you'll invariably be asked if you want a **short then**. Another little tip before you head off to the pub section in the Entertainment chapter is that there's no such thing as 'a half' when ordering beer here. There's a **pint** or a **glass** (half

---

THE WORKMAN'S FRIEND

The poem below was written by Flann O'Brien, the pseudonym of Brian O'Nolan (1911–66), in *At Swim Two Birds*. *A pint of plain is your only man* is one of his famous quotations, meaning 'a pint of stout will solve all your problems'.

When things go wrong and will not come right,
Though you do the best you can,
When life looks black as the hour of night –
A pint of plain is your only man.

When money's tight and is hard to get
And your horse has also ran,
When all you have is a heap of debt –
A pint of plain is your only man.

When health is bad and your heart feels strange,
And your face is pale and wan,
When doctors say that you need a change,
A pint of plain is your only man.

When food is scarce and your larder bare
And no rashers grease your pan,
When hunger grows as your meals are rare –
A pint of plain is your only man.

In time of trouble and lousy strife,
You have still got a darlint plan,
You still can turn to a brighter life –
A pint of plain is your only man.

a pint). After a big feed, when you can't stomach a beer, there are plenty of notable Irish liqueurs to keep you company. **Baileys Original Irish Cream** is the one you're probably already familiar with, but there's also **Carolans**.

But perhaps the drink that says most about this wonderful country is whiskey, or *the cratur* as it's known around these parts (the word is, rather obscurely, an Elizabethan pronunciation of 'creature'). Every sip of Irish whiskey has behind it an encyclopedia of Irish life and history, and the offer of a *dram* (a measure of whiskey) is on page one of the Irish guide to hospitality. The modern drink is derived from the illegal one which was widely made by peasant cottage distilleries, known as *poitín* (Irish for 'little pot', pronounced *puh·*cheen). When the British occupied Ireland, they decided to start taxing the drink and made it legal. The larger distillers cosied up to the authorities, and taxes from their whiskey lined the pockets of the British exchequer. Their spirit came to be known colloquially as **Parliament whiskey**.

GENERAL DRINKING TERMS

If you want to get on the *gargle* (alcohol) when in Ireland, you'd best take note of the following vocabulary:

Arthur Scargill	rhyming slang for a *gargle* (drink); named after the Miners' Union leader in the '80s in England
baby power	a miniature bottle of **Powers Irish Whiskey** (the favoured size for a handbag)
barrack buster	a large two-litre bottle, usually of cider
blue peter	two-litre flagon of cider
drink link	an ATM
drop	a small amount of drink (relatively speaking) – after 10 pints, it's time to take it easy: *Just a drop, thanks*
flagon	large two-litre bottle, usually of cider
gargle	alcohol – used as a verb it means 'to go out drinking'
gatt	alcohol (Cork)
hard stuff/tack	neat spirits (usually whiskey)

jar	a drink, usually used in the plural – *Do ye fancy a coupla jars?*
naggin	a small bottle of spirits that fits into an inside coat pocket
rozziner	the hair of the dog (a hangover cure)
scoop	an amount of drink – *How about a few scoops?*
shorts	neat spirits (usually whiskey)
Sláinte!	(pronounced *slawn*·cha) Cheers! – literally 'health' in Irish
slug	a mouthful – usually used between kids as in *Gis a slug!*
straightener	the hair of the dog (a hangover cure)

the Angel's Share the whiskey that evaporates from the barrels during the maturation period between five and 12 years. The phrase was probably coined by the first guy caught copying the keys to the warehouse.

the Demon Drink a phrase first coined in the mid-19th century by a famous Capuchin friar, Father Matthew Theobald, who campaigned around the country trying quite successfully to get people off the drink. Alcoholism was widespread at the time.

fat frog a mixture of three alcopops (alcoholic ice-blocks) – WKD Blue, Smirnoff Ice and Bacardi Breezer – all thrown into a pint glass. The colour comes out a light green. Strictly for the kids.

WHERE WHISKEY GOT ITS NAME

When whiskey was first made by the monks in Ireland they knew they were on to a good thing and called it *uisce beatha* (Irish for 'water of life', pronounced *ish*·ka *ba*·ha). Non-Irish speakers, particularly parched English soldiers stationed in Ireland, couldn't wrap their heads around the local words (even before they'd had a few) and anglicised it to *whiskey*. However, nobody knows whether they meant it with an *e* or not – only the Irish spell it this way.

Gilroy John Gilroy, the artist responsible for the most famous *Guinness* advertising posters from the 1930s and 1940s, which featured all sorts of animals and slogans like *My Goodness My Guinness* and *Guinness Makes You Strong*. You'll see these on pub walls all over Ireland and they've become collector's items.

hot toddy a miracle cure for a cold (and a good excuse to keep drinking even when you've got a cold), this is whiskey mixed with boiling water, cloves, lemon and an optional spoon of sugar

lock in less likely to happen these days because of more relaxed licensing laws which allow pubs to stay open later, but this used to be the highlight of the evening. The landlord would lock the doors at closing time, dim the lights and pretend (to any passing police) that the pub was closed.

Paddy's the most popular whiskey in Munster, which originally went by the catchy name *Cork Distilleries Company Old Irish Whiskey*. It was sold by a popular chap named Paddy Flaherty who used to ride around the place delivering supplies on his bicycle. When pubs ran out, they'd send word to the distillery that they needed more of Paddy's whiskey: hence the name.

Pioneers although the Irish reputation for drinking is well founded, some 50,000 of them, mostly older folk, won't let a drop of alcohol pass their lips. They're members of the *Pioneer Total Abstinence Association*, established in Dublin in 1898. They're called *pioneers* and are vaguely mistrusted by the general populace. They claim they're not so much anti-alcohol as pro-sobriety and wear lapel pins bearing an image of the sacred heart, devotion to which is encouraged to help them resist temptation.

YER ONLY MAN

The word *arthurs* refers to *Guinness* and comes from the name of the legendary founder Arthur Guinness. Stout in general is called *the black stuff*. Punters sometimes order a pint of *plain* or *porter*, but you'll most commonly order a *pint*. Try it – even with your accent, the barman will invariably presume you mean the local stout.

While some will baulk at the notion of mixing stout with anything but oysters, there are a couple of popular exceptions. *Black velvet* is as smooth as it sounds, and combines stout and champagne, while a *black and tan* – named after the auxiliary force sent over by the British during Ireland's War of Independence – is half ale and half stout.

The purists will really pick on you for any of the following combinations, although they are requested from time to time. A *baby Guinness* is half *Baileys* and half *Guinness* in a shot glass; a *stout and black* is a pint with a couple of drops of blackcurrant cordial, which sweetens the drink somewhat – it's usually drunk by women and teenagers trying to wean themselves onto the hard stuff. A *Johnny-jump-up* mixes *Guinness* and cider.

poteen (pronounced *puh*·cheen). The anglicised spelling of *poitín*, illegal Irish whiskey or moonshine. Usually made from grain or potatoes (also colloquially called *Paddy's eyewater*).

red lemonade a red-coloured lemonade which is a popular mixer in combinations such as a *Paddy and red* (with *Paddy's whiskey*) or *Suddy and red*, (mixed with Southern Comfort liquor). A non-alcoholic combination features a pint glass filled with ice, lemonade and Red Bull – a potent little number known as a *kick in the bollocks*. It's a rites of passage thing for Irish youngsters the first time they're abroad (usually in England) to ask for something *and red*. The bartender, perplexed, might ask 'With Ribena?' (a brand of blackcurrant cordial).

supping up time the half-hour you have, officially, between buying your drink at last orders and leaving the premises *a wee dram*   a measure of whiskey. A *dram*'s a *dram* but it makes people feel like they're not drinking as much if they precede it with the word *wee*.

TEA BREAK

When it comes to refreshment, tea (or *Rosie Lee* in Irish rhyming slang) is paramount in Ireland, and much more popular than coffee. In fact, the Irish drink more tea (pronounced *tay* in the North) per capita than any other nation. The drinking and sharing of tea is inextricably linked with Irish sociability and the offer of a *cha*, a *cuppa* or a *cuppa cha* is the first expression of Irish hospitality in the home. If you haven't experienced how insistent Irish mothers can be and how they like to fuss over guests, just try and refuse the offer of tea. The conversation might go something like this:

—*Are you for a cuppa?*
—Sorry?
—*Will you have a cup of tea?*
—No thanks.
—*Ah, of course you will.*
—No, really I don't want any tea.
—*You will, you will, you will, you will. You will. Ah go on.*
—No tea.
—*Sure, I'm just after putting the kettle on and everyone else is having one.*
—I don't drink tea.
—*You don't drink tea! Course you drink tea, now have a cup.*
—Honestly, no. And you're kind of scaring me now.
—*Go on, go on, go on, go on. You don't drink tea, HA!*
—It makes me feel sick.
—*Ah, will you cad yourself on. You'll have a cup of tea, just a cup in your hand.*

And that's a compromise. The *cup in your hand* is the very least you can do. It's in your hand because you're not at the more formal table setting and you might be standing or in a rush.

There are a few more words and phrases associated with the ritual of tea drinking in Ireland:

be mother   when the tea in the pot is just about infused, someone will offer or be asked to **be mother**, ie pour the tea into everyone's cup

Bewleys   an Irish institution: a chain of quaint tearooms that have gone the way of 'progress', and now only survive in one tearoom and lots of memories

draw; **steep**   what the water does in the pot while it's becoming tea

tea you could dance on/stand a spoon in   stewed (over-infused) tea which tastes unpleasantly strong – you've ruined it basically

wet the tea   make tea (ie wet the leaves in the bottom of the pot)

IRISH COFFEE

Only Irish coffee provides in a single glass all four essential food groups: alcohol, caffeine, sugar, and fat.
—Alex Levine

Much more popular outside Ireland than within, *Irish Coffee* (the sweet combination of coffee and your favourite whiskey) was created by Joe Sheridan, a bartender at Ireland's Shannon Airport. It was his response to the constant requests he got from shivering tourists passing through and looking for something alcoholic that would also warm them up. This is his winning formula:

Irish coffee

1 jigger (about 50ml) of whiskey
1 teaspoon sugar
1–2 tablespoons chilled, whipped (or double) cream
1 cup strong, hot coffee

Method

Warm a stemmed whiskey glass with hot water. Add coffee and stir in sugar until it's dissolved (necessary in order for the cream to float). Add whiskey. Pour the cream, very gently, over the back of a teaspoon onto the drink so it has a rich, velvety creamy head. And serve without excuse.

Nutmeg, cinnamon, or another spice may be added, but are not usual. An alternative version, more properly known as *Baileys coffee*, adds a shot (ounce) of *Baileys Irish Cream*, to the mix, or replace the whiskey altogether. The original has inspired many other pretenders, and now you can find coffee combined with all sorts of different liqueurs, under the guise of fancy names like *royale coffee* (with Cognac) or *calypso coffee* (with Tia Maria). Needless to say you wouldn't be such a philistine as to request any of these in Ireland.

The Irish – both men and women – are mad keen sports fans, whether they're playing the games themselves, supporting their teams from the stands or shouting at them from their bar stools. And let's be charitable, the proliferation of football (soccer) and *GAA* (Gaelic Athletic Association) jerseys on the shoulders of the younger generation says more about their passion for sport than their wayward fashion sense.

Football, in one form or another, dominates the Irish sporting scene. It's been said that *rugby is a thug's game played by gentlemen, soccer is a gentleman's game played by thugs and Gaelic games are thugs' games played by thugs*. The native games of *Gaelic football* and *hurling* are the most popular sports in Ireland, though. Along with *camogie* (women's *hurling*), *Ladies' Gaelic football*, *Gaelic handball* and *rounders* (a bat-and-ball game similar to softball), they make up the national sports of Ireland, collectively known as *Gaelic games*.

Many sports, such as rugby, *Gaelic football* and *hurling*, are organised on an all-island basis, with a single team representing Ireland in international competitions. Others, like soccer, have separate organising bodies in Northern Ireland and the Republic of Ireland. At the Olympics, a person from Northern Ireland can choose to represent either the Ireland or the Great Britain team.

Gaelic games

The ancient *Gaelic games* are at the very core of Irishness and enmeshed in the fabric of community life. When the *GAA* was established in 1884 and clubs were set up around the country, training often took the form of military exercises to help volunteer independence fighters get fit and marshalled. A spike in the popularity of *Gaelic games* went hand in hand with a broader Gaelic revival during a time when Ireland's struggle for independence was gathering momentum. It warms the heart to see that, despite globalisation and the general commercialisation of sport, the entirely amateur games of *Gaelic football* and *hurling* are still far and away the most popular sports in the country.

The headquarters of the *GAA* (and the main *Gaelic games* stadium) is located at the hallowed ground of *Croke Park* in central Dublin, which has a capacity of 82,500. (It's the fourth-largest stadium in Europe – astonishing for a ground that hosts sports that are almost entirely limited to Ireland.) *Croke Park* hosts the home games of Dublin teams as well as the national semi-finals in *hurling*, *Gaelic football* and *camogie*. The championship season climaxes at *Croke Park* on the first Sunday of September, when the two best county *hurling* teams on the island battle it out for the *Liam McCarthy Cup*. On the fourth Sunday of September the two *Gaelic football* finalists battle it out in the *All-Ireland Final* for the *Sam Maguire Cup*. The *camogie* and *women's Gaelic football* finals are usually held on the weekends between the *hurling* and *Gaelic football* finals.

The *GAA* club is the heart and soul of every parish in the country, and its teams command support from most of the community. The fiercest rivalries are often between clubs in neighbouring parishes, but when the best players from the clubs are selected to play for the county, local rivalries are put aside and replaced by intercounty ones as supporters unite behind their county colours. As passionate and intense as the rivalries are, there's rarely a cross word between fans, who are ultimately united behind the games and their shared heritage.

GAELIC FOOTBALL

Gaelic football is clearly the greatest game on earth, bar none – just ask any Irish person. It combines athleticism, speed, strength, aggression, skill, grace and intelligence. To really get a feel for the game you probably need to go along to a match with some locals who can *fill you in on* (explain) the details, but following is a brief synopsis of the rules.

Gaelic football teams consist of 15 players and matches have two 35-minute halves. The ball is round like a soccer ball and the players can pass it by kicking or *fisting* (handballing) it in any direction to other players on the run. Players can also carry the ball while running, but not for more than four steps unless they bounce it or kick it and then retrieve it. Players are not allowed to pick the ball up directly from the ground. Tackling is generally more robust than in soccer but is gentler than in rugby. The excitement of the game is enhanced by the ducking and weaving feinting manoeuvres of players attempting to wrong-foot their opponents.

The goalposts are similar to H-shaped rugby posts but have a net at the bottom. A goal, worth three points, is scored by putting the ball into the net, while a single point is awarded when the ball goes over the bar. If a team scores two goals and 11 points, the score would be written as 2–11 and called out as *two eleven*, which would be the equivalent of 17 points. County Kerry, also known as *the Kingdom*, is clearly the best team in the country with a record haul of 33 *All-Ireland Championships* to its name. Its closest rivals are Dublin, Meath, Cork and, of late, Tyrone.

HURLING

Hurling is the other main *Gaelic game*. It's a ferocious 15-a-side sport played with a *hurley* (a long stick with a flattish blade) and a *sliothar* (a small leather ball a little smaller than a cricket ball or baseball). The goalposts and scoring methods are the same as in *Gaelic football*. A player can pick up the ball and run with it for a certain distance. Players can handle the ball briefly and pass it by palming it.

Hurling is the fastest field game in the world and demands superb skill, lightning speed and a complete and total lack of fear. There are few sounds more likely to make your blood curdle – or aficionados drool – than the so-called *clash of the ash* (*hurleys* are traditionally made from the root of the ash tree) when the sticks of two *hurlers* collide at full tilt. Amazingly, protective helmets are not compulsory; even more amazingly, serious injuries are few.

Hurling dates back to ancient times and the mythical Celtic hero *Cuchulainn* was said to have been a handy *left corner-forward*. The game is most popular outside Dublin. In fact, *Dubs* (Dubliners) call it a *culchie* (country bumpkin) sport unless their team actually wins a game, and then it's the *fastest bleeding field game in the wuurrld*. Wexford, Galway, Cork, Kilkenny and Tipperary are the powerhouses of the game. The equally tough women's version *camogie*, has been promoted in recent years (somewhat disturbingly) under the slogan *chicks with sticks*.

GAELIC HANDBALL & ROUNDERS

Gaelic handball is another code governed by the *GAA* and another sport with ancient origins. It's somewhat similar to squash or racquetball, the difference being that the ball is hit with a gloved hand rather than a racquet. Unlike the Olympic version of the sport, it's played by two individuals or two pairs. *Gaelic handball* was once very popular but has been declining somewhat in recent decades.

Rounders is a bat-and-ball game similar to softball, where teams try to score *rounders* (points) by completing a circle of posts.

THE LINGO

Gaelic games are full-blooded affairs and, as you might expect, so is much of the language. Below is a summary of common terms relating to the games as well as some commonly heard exclamations:

Ah come on to fuck wilya!	a common exclamation from an exasperated fan
Burst the bollix!	an instruction to tackle a player from the opposing team

Clatter	tackle the man before he
da fecker!	runs through and scores
hames	a right mess – as in *He made a hames of that clearance*
hatchet man	a rough player, usually in the team for his Neanderthal instincts
hill 16	a famous stand at *Croke Park*, where Dublin fans always congregate and chant
joult	a push – as in *I gave him a joult and now he has to wear a neck brace*
mighty	very good
minors	the under-18's
***mullocker*;**	an untidy but rough player let
mullocks	loose for matches – fewer brains than a ***hatchet man*** but capable of striking fear into the opposition
namajaysus	an expression of indignation – perhaps shorthand for *What was that free for, referee?*
pull	in *hurling*, when a player hits the ball from the ground
timber	a term used to intimidate a *hurling* opponent, as in *Show him some timber!*
welt	to swing hard at the ball in *hurling*
ya-bollix-ya	a corner-back's formal acknowledgment of a score by his opponent

Artane Boys' Band   officially the *Artane Band* now, because girls are allowed to join, this traditional marching band is synonymous with *Croke Park* and plays before, and during half-time, at every big match. U2 drummer Larry Mullen is a former member.

GAA the Gaelic Athletic Association, the governing body for *Gaelic games* (sometimes pronounced 'gaa' as if it were a word when used in reference to Gaelic football)

hockeyed/leathered them out of it beat them soundly

junior nothing to do with age: a division for players who are either past it or not good enough to get into the *senior* team. You get all shapes and sizes playing *junior football* and *hurling.*

Leh it in ta feck would ya! a *full-forward's* appeal to a *mid-fielder* to stop prancing about and just send the ball to him

Man on! or **Mind yer house!** warnings from fans to players that they're about to be tackled, usually from behind

rule 42 the controversial *GAA* rule that prohibits 'foreign' (read 'English') games being played at *GAA* grounds. In practice it's applied primarily to soccer and rugby – an American football game was played at *Croke Park* in the 1980s. This rule was suspended in 2005 to allow soccer and rugby internationals to be played there while *Landsdowne Road* (the traditional home of soccer and rugby) was being rebuilt.

running row a dispute between players that continues on from the pitch to the dressing rooms to the car park to the pub to the next time the two teams play

schkelp to remove living tissue in the absence of a surgical procedure, as in *That shite from Tipp* (Tipperary) *took a schkelp outta me leg*

Football (soccer)

There's huge support for the 'World Game' in Ireland. The domestic competitions are the *League of Ireland* in the Republic and the *Irish Football League* in Northern Ireland. Fans, however, are much more enthusiastic about teams in the English and Scottish Premier Leagues than they are about the poor, mostly part-time sods rolling around in the mud as part of the struggling domestic competitions.

All of Ireland's top footballers ply their trade in the British leagues, which only makes it more difficult for the indigenous competitions to get a look-in. On the international front, though, the Republic of Ireland had an amazing run of it throughout the '80s and early '90s, reaching the final stages of the European championships in 1988 and the World Cup in 1990 and 1994. Since then the team has had a massive following, even though there's been little to cheer about of late. Northern Ireland hasn't been in a major competition since its heroics in the World Cup in Spain in 1982.

The national body in the Republic is the *FAI* (*Football Association of Ireland*); in Northern Ireland there's the *IFA* (*Irish Football Association*). Maybe, just maybe, if they got together to form an all-Ireland team they might see a lift in their performances and stop being so crap. The venue for international matches in the South is Dublin's **Landsdowne Road** stadium. The Northern Ireland football team plays its internationals at Belfast's **Windsor Park**.

TEAMS – REPUBLIC OF IRELAND

Following are the names of the seventeen teams that play as part of the *Eircom League* in the Republic of Ireland. The Irish inventiveness with English is reflected in the proliferation of nicknames attached to the teams.

TEAM	NICKNAME
Athletic	no nickname we're aware of
Bohemians	the Bohs; the Gypos; the Gypsies
Bray Wanderers	the Seagulls
Cork City	the City; the Leesiders; the Rebel Army
Derry City	the Candy Stripes
Drogheda United	the Drogs

Dublin City FC	CHF; the Vikings – (the former nickname is used by other teams and supporters to mock them. It stands for *Continuity Home Farm* – *Home Farm* being the original club that they grew out of.)
Dundalk	fans of their neighbours, Drogheda, mock them using the name 'Craptown'
Finn Harps	the Harps; the Sheep Shaggers
Galway United	the Westlanders
Longford Town	De Town; the Town
St Patrick's	the Junkies; the (Saint) Pats; the Supersaints
Shamrock Rovers	the Hoops; the Rovers; Scumrock; the Shams (the last two being derogatory)
Shelbourne	the Real Reds; the Shels
Sligo Rovers	Bit o' Red; the Rovers
UCD	the College; the Students
Waterford United	the Blues

TEAMS – NORTHERN IRELAND
There are nine teams in the *Irish Premier League* of Northern Ireland:

TEAM	NICKNAME
Ballymena	the Sky Blues
Bangor	the Seagulls
Cliftonville FC	the Reds
Coleraine FC	the Bansiders
Distillery FC	no nickname we're aware of
Glentoran FC	the Cock 'n' Hens; the Glens
Linfield FC	the Blues; the Lins
Lisburn	the Whites
Portadown FC	the Ports

FAMOUS IRISH FOOTBALLERS

George Best

The greatest footballer to come out of Ireland. He lived the high life on and off the pitch, and remained in the spotlight long after his playing days were over – partly because of his alcoholism, which caused his premature death in late 2005 at the age of 59. Famously, he once said 'I spent a fortune on women, gambling and drink – the rest I just squandered.' Another time, when facing a prison sentence for drink-driving and failing to appear in court, he turned to his defence team and dejected friends before sentencing and said, 'I suppose that's the knighthood fucked then.' RIP.

Liam Brady

A sublimely talented left-footed midfielder during the '70s and '80s and one of the greatest players to have ever donned an Irish jersey. He blazed a trail for British-based footballers by fashioning a successful career for himself in the glamour league of Serie A in Italy. Unfortunately, his international career ended just before the Ireland team's modest successes in the '80s and early '90s.

Jack Charlton

World Cup winner with England. He also became the first non-Irish manager of the Republic of Ireland from 1987–96 and led the team to unparalleled success with industrial tactics and a canny stretching of the eligibility rules.

Roy Keane

A great player haunted by his own demons. Caused a sporting civil war in Ireland in 2002 when he walked out on the Irish team on the eve of the World Cup, complaining about a lack of professionalism. Also abruptly parted with his club Manchester United in late 2005, citing not very much at all. He's now the manager of Sunderland in the English championship.

Martin O'Neill

Capped 62 times for Northern Ireland and captain of the team in their historic World Cup campaign in Spain in 1982. He went on to become a very successful manager, first during a five-year stint at Celtic and then at Aston Villa.

Rugby

Although traditionally the preserve of the upper and middle classes, rugby captures the attention of the whole island in spring during the major international competition, the *Six Nations Championship*. That's because the Ireland team is drawn from both sides of the border and is supported by *Nationalists* as well as *Unionists*. In recognition of this spirit, the sport's governing body – the *IRFU* (Irish Rugby Football Union) – replaced the fervently nationalistic (and militaristic) national anthem of the Republic, *The Soldier's Call*, with the neutral *Ireland's Call* which is played before international games these days.

The *Six Nations Championship* is contested by Ireland, England, Wales, Scotland, Italy and France. If either the British or Irish team beats the other three teams, it wins the *Triple Crown*. The team that triumphs over all the others wins the *Grand Slam*; whoever finishes last gets the dreaded *Wooden Spoon*.

Rugby is commonly played throughout Ireland, but is especially popular in Munster (County Limerick is known as the home of Irish rugby) and Ulster in Northern Ireland. Rugby is played at club, province and national levels. Throughout most of the rest of the rugby-playing world, there's a battle between two codes, union and league, but no league is played in Ireland.

IRISH RUGBY PERSONALITIES

Ollie Campbell

He hasn't played for a couple of decades but deserves his place as Ireland's most legendary No 10. Among his heroic feats, in 1984 he kicked all of Ireland's 21 points against Scotland to secure the country's first *Triple Crown* since 1948.

Brian O'Driscoll

Captain and poster boy of the Irish team although it's had little to celebrate in recent years. He's a tremendously gifted *outside centre* who excites every time he gets the ball. He captained the *British Lions* (a team drawn from the four teams of the British Isles) in 2005.

The rules are relatively simple. All you need to know to start following the game is that there are 15 players on each team, and the winner is the team that scores the most **points** by getting the oval-shaped ball over their opponents' line – either by touching it down in play for a **try** (worth four points) or kicking it through the posts for a **drop goal** (three points). After a **try**, the team also gets the opportunity to kick the ball at the posts from a position parallel to where the **try** was scored. This is called a **conversion** and is worth two points. Tackling above the shoulders is prohibited.

The ball can be kicked forward or thrown behind to a teammate. When a player either deliberately or inadvertently moves the ball forward with his hands, a **free** (free kick) is awarded to the other team for what's known as a **knock on**. A **line-out** occurs when the ball goes out of play and is thrown back in by the referee between two lines of opponents. Broadly, a **scrum** is an organised struggle between opposing **packs** (of players) trying to gain ground while the ball is on the ground. A **ruck** is like a **scrum** that just occurs naturally in play.

Horse racing

A passion for horse racing is deeply entrenched in Irish life and comes without the snobbery of its English counterpart. There are some 25 racecourses in the Republic of Ireland and two in Northern Ireland, which should give you some idea of just how popular the sport is. The racing in Ireland is first class and the country has a venerable tradition of breeding and training great thoroughbred race horses. A day at the **horses**, **nags** or **gee gees** or at the **trots** (harness races) in Ireland is one to remember fondly – so long as you don't **lose your shirt** (lose big on your bets). Given the seriousness with which enthusiasts take their gambling, you could be forgiven for wondering whether horse racing should be classed as an affliction rather than a sport. Here are a few terms related to horse racing:

flat races	races without jumps
jumps	races in which horses negotiate jumps
punter	someone who bets on the horses
steeplechase	a race with a series of obstacles in the form of fences and ditches
still running	what someone will say if the horse they bet on was no good
turf accountant	a *bookie* or *betting shop* for horse or greyhound racing
won a few bob	what someone will say if they've won big – if pressed, they'll revert to *broke even* (see below)

book running a *book* is the act of quoting odds and accepting bets on an event. Hence the terms *bookie* and *bookmaker*.

broke even what a *punter* will invariably tell their spouse when they ask whether they won or lost on the races. Miraculously, despite the fact that gambling on horses is supposed to be a multimillion euro business in Ireland, no money ever seems to change hands.

Greyhound racing

Greyhound racing was first established in Ireland, North and South, in 1927. Traditionally the poor man's punt, *greyhound racing* has enjoyed something of a resurgence in popularity in recent years, thanks partly to corporate interest in *going to the dogs*.

There are 20 licensed tracks, and the annual *Paddy Power Irish Greyhound Derby*, held in August at *Shelbourne Park* in Dublin, is one of the richest greyhound races in the world. Dogs are generally owned by syndicates. Prize money ranges from a few hundred euros to several thousand for top races.

The great *Mick the Miller*, winner of the English Derby in 1929 and 1930, was an Irish greyhound and Ireland continues to breed and export racing greyhounds.

Other sports

There's a big drop-off in popularity between the sports mentioned above and other sports in Ireland. Nevertheless, other sports enjoy their own niche support and the Irish will watch any sport so long as it's exciting.

ATHLETICS

Middle- and long-distance running is a favourite in Ireland, and the country has produced many elite runners over the years. For examples, the great *Ron Delaney* (Olympic gold medallist over 800m in 1956), *Eamon Coughlan* (an indoor specialist nicknamed the *Chairman of the Boards* and world champion over 5000m in 1983), *John Treacy* (Olympic silver medallist in the marathon in 1984), four-time cross-country world silver medallist *Catriona McKiernan* and *Sonia O'Sullivan*, the greatest Irish track runner of the modern (drug-tainted) era, former world-record holder and world champion over 5000m (1995). Despite its illustrious past, athletics is struggling to get media attention and corporate sponsorship these days.

BOXING

Irish boxers also have an excellent record, winning many Olympic medals over the years and turning out some very decent pros, including former world champion *Barry Mc-Guigan*, Olympic silver medallist *Wayne McCullough* from Northern Ireland and middleweight champions *Stephen*

Collins and *Michael Carruth*, an Olympic gold medallist from the South. *Francie Barret* (a *Traveller*) famously carried the flag and boxed for Ireland at the 1996 Atlanta Olympics.

CYCLING

Although the glory days of Irish cycling have receded, the sport is still very popular in Ireland, which famously hosted a stage of the Tour de France in 1998.

There are several regional clubs throughout the country and several competitions are organised regularly, such as the *Rás* (*rás* is the Irish for 'race'), one of the longest-surviving stage races in Europe.

One of Ireland's most famous cycling sons is *Stephen Roche*, who took out the trifecta of the Tour de France, the Giro d'Italia and the World Championships in 1987 to record one of the greatest moments in Irish sporting history. Another hero is Tipperary's *Sean Kelly*, who won the sprinter's green jersey in the Tour de France four times and the Vuelta a España in 1988, and was a lovely bloke with an accent so thick that not even his compatriots could understand him.

GOLF

Ireland has long been renowned for its outstanding golf courses, particularly the links (coastal courses), and golf tourism has grown rapidly in recent years. It hosts several prestigious events and is a production line for many outstanding players, including recent stars *Padraig Harrington*, *Darren Clarke* and *Paul McGinley*. There was a legal kerfuffle a few years ago about women not being admitted as members of certain clubs. The Irish Equality Authority lost its case against Portmarnock Golf Club in 2004 seeking to have women admitted as members.

SHOWJUMPING

Equestrian sports are generally the preserve of the *horsey set*, but much of the country sits up to take notice during the annual international *Dublin Horse Show* at the *Royal Dublin*

Showgrounds. Because of its long equestrian heritage, Ireland has always done better than a country its size really should at showjumping. But the reputation of the country was seriously damaged after Olympic medal winner *Cian O'Connor* was exposed as a drug cheat after the 2004 Athens Olympics.

SWIMMING

It's amazing that in such a small island, where you're never too far from the sea, so many Irish people can't swim at all. If you've ever gone for a *dip* (swim) in the icy-cold oceans that lap the island perhaps you won't be so surprised. This fact – and the not-inconsiderable obstacle that there wasn't a single Olympic-size swimming pool in the country until 2001 – didn't stop Irish-born (Dutch-trained) swimmer *Michelle Smith* from coming out of nowhere to scoop three gold medals

and a bronze at the Atlanta Olympics in 1996 at the relatively mature age of 26. More amazing still was the fairly muted response back home, where any sort of medal would normally be met with an open-top bus tour and a civic reception. Many weren't surprised when a few years later she was found to have tampered with a doping sample, which the white coats said contained more whiskey than any human could possibly handle. She was disgraced and largely air-brushed from Irish sporting folklore.

COMMUNITY GAMES

Ireland's passion for sport is on display at the *Community Games*, a big multi-sport event organised at the local level. It gives hundreds of thousands of young people the opportunity to participate with and compete against kids from their neighbourhoods in a number of disciplines including athletics, swimming and cycling. Winners progress to county level, and then on to the *Community Games Finals*, which are held over two weekends in summer every year.

The world already knows that the Irish love nothing better than a *bit of craic* (a bit of fun, pronounced 'crack'). Entertaining, and being entertained, are more than mere pastimes for the Irish: they're the social fabric that binds and defines the communities to which they belong.

Foreigners who are used to thinking of entertainment in Ireland as centred around the pub are surprised to learn that there's plenty of nightlife beyond the pub. In fact, there's plenty to do, whatever your tastes, and Ireland is bursting with cultural expression from classical theatre to Hollywood *flicks* (movies), from wicked comedy to cutting-edge music to frenetic dance clubs to spectacular sport. Whatever it is that *floats your boat* you're sure to find a version of it in Ireland. And a little more besides.

That said, the Irish themselves are often quite content with just warm company and good cheer. Of course, if the mood takes them this can lead to what the Irish affectionately call a *session* (generally a time of drink and good cheer, though the word can also refer to a *session* of traditional music). If everything falls into place, there may even be a *hooley* (a great, lively party with singing, dancing and yet more drinking). But it all starts at the iconic Irish pub, one of the country's most legendary exports, and where visitors to Ireland are likely to experience some of the highlights of their trip.

The Irish pub

Too young to die. Too drunk to live.
—Renee McCall of the *Daily Express* on the passing of the writer Brendan Behan in 1964 at the age of 41

The pub is the great leveller in Ireland, where status and rank have no meaning, where generation gaps are bridged, inhibitions dropped, tongues loosened, schemes hatched, songs sung, stories told and gossip embroidered. It's a national institution: at once a theatre and a cosy room, a centre stage and a hideaway, a debating chamber and a place of silent contemplation. Above all, though, it has been a solace for a frequently harsh reality.

Talk – be it frivolous, earnest or incoherent – is the essential ingredient at a pub. Once the cogs of conversation have been oiled you can end up being transported into an entirely different realm. The Irish love a chat, and even asking a run-of-the-mill tourist question could mean that you end up with a lifelong friend.

Brace yourself, though, because banter is the language of choice, and **slagging** (teasing) over a few **jars** (drinks) is another national pastime. Newcomers might judge the exchanges caustic but they'll soon become aware that everyone takes it in good part. The front bar is normally where the regulars hang out and where you'll hear the most **slagging**. There are often only a few tables and most **punters** (customers) stand at the bar (also known as the **counter**). Most pubs also have a **lounge**, which was originally the place for women and families and is designed to accommodate groups sitting around tables. In most pubs you can get **pub grub**, staple fare being main meals such as steak, lasagne and shepherd's pie, all accompanied by the ubiquitous **chips**.

Strangely, while entrepreneurs around the globe are trying to recreate the atmosphere of an Irish pub, new Dublin bars are trying to emulate drinking holes found elsewhere in the world. A real Irish pub – a traditional pub in Ireland, as opposed to the franchised version exported around the world – is essentially low-key, without **diddly-I** (sentimentally Irish) paraphernalia, and a place where people make their own entertainment. As you'll soon realise, bricks and mortar do not an Irish pub make and it's the spirit of the people and the culture that make it special.

PUB PRACTICALITIES

Licensing laws governing drinking hours have been relaxed in recent years, and in big towns and cities you won't have any trouble drinking your way into the *wee hours* of the morning. *Down the country* (outside Dublin) you may still come across the *late lock-in*, where instead of kicking you out at closing time the landlord closes the doors and dims the lights, to give the outside world the impression that the pub is closed while carrying on surreptitiously serving.

If you're *gumming* (desperately thirsty) for a drink, with a little effort you can get one any time of the day or night. Many clubs stay open until 4 or 5 in the morning; if you're clubbed out you can always track down *early bird pubs* that cater to market porters, postal workers and the like.

Pubs used to be forced to close for a couple of hours in the afternoon, essentially to discourage people from drinking the whole day away. This was called the *holy hour*, although it usually lasted for two and although some pubs still maintain the tradition, it's no longer required by law. On some religious holidays – like Good Friday – the pubs and clubs will open at midnight, as you can't drink on *holy days*. As soon as midnight strikes, piety is put aside and the towns come alive!

In all pubs you pay for your drinks when you get them – not when you leave. Usually you go to the bar yourself, although many quieter, more family-oriented pubs will have *lounge boys* or *lounge girls*, who take orders from tables. At quiet times, these guys usually double up as *glassies* or *glass boys* or *girls*, fetching glasses from the tables. It's customary to tip them when you pay. If you're ordering all your drinks from the bartender, it's not uncommon to buy him or her a drink from time to time. Just say *and one for yourself* when you've finished your order.

Ireland was one of the first countries to ban smoking in public places, but it shocked many in 2004 when it went ahead and banned smoking in both restaurants and the cherished pub! *Joe Public* never thought it would work, that there'd be a mutiny, but it has. Some women joke (or are they serious?) that they preferred it when smoking was allowed because all you can smell in pubs these days are men's farts.

PUB ETIQUETTE

The most important thing you must bring to an Irish pub is an at-least rudimentary grasp of the *rounds system*, which is the bedrock of Irish drinking culture. It's based on the simple custom that when somebody buys you a drink you buy one back. Hence the old Irish saying *It's impossible for two men to go for one drink*.

The Irish are a forgiving lot but nothing will hasten your fall from grace like the failure to uphold the pub law of *shouting* (buying a drink) when it's your turn. To an outsider, the *rounds system* may appear to be very casual. You might not be told when it's your round and others may appear only too happy to stand in for you. But make no mistake, your failure to *put your hand in your pocket* will be noticed. People will mention it the minute you leave the room, probably dismissing you with one of the worst put-downs in the local vernacular: *a mean bastard*. The dishonour will follow you to the grave, following which it will attach to your children and possibly theirs as well. In the worst cases, it may become permanently enshrined in a family nickname. Friendly reminders that it's your turn to *shout* include: *The tide's going out*; *It's your round!* or the less subtle *Get the bleedin' gargle in!*

The best thing to do is to err on the side of generosity. It's highly unlikely that an Irish person would take advantage of you in this case because the guilt would be too much for them to bear. As long as you show a willingness to abide by the rules you'll be *grand* (all right). Just bear in mind that the *round* is due as soon as the quickest drinker has finished (or is preferably *about* to finish) their drink. It doesn't matter if you're not even halfway through yours.

Every time you buy a *round*, you should say *Same again*, which is half question and half statement. If you're *skint* or *brassock* (have no money) you should opt out of the first *round* and give your reasons. You can't accept an invitation into the *round* and then opt out when you're *in the chair* (it's your turn to buy). If the group think you're genuine, they might *sponsor* (pay for) you anyway. But if you're trying to pull a fast one, they'll pick you for a *chancer* (someone who's false) straight away. When someone else is buying a *round* in which you rightfully should be included, it doesn't matter if you have a *clatter* (an undetermined number) of drinks in front of you, they'll most likely buy another for you anyway. If they decide that a new drink will have gone flat by the time you've caught up, they'll most likely *leave one in* for you, which means they've paid for the drink and the barman will pour it when you're ready.

CROWN BAR, BELFAST

One of Ireland's most famous pubs is the *Crown Bar* in Great Victoria Street, Belfast. It's a triumph of Victorian architecture with a colourful exterior clad in faience and tiles and a sumptuous interior boasting carved snugs, an ornate bar and decorative floors and ceilings. This watering hole is popular with locals and tourists alike.

Legend has it that when the bar was built there was a dispute between the husband and wife proprietors over calling it the Crown. The wife, who was a Protestant, chose the name but her Catholic husband objected to adopting a symbol of the British regime. In the end, the husband stipulated that if his wife got her way, he should be allowed to have a mosaic crown installed on the floor at the entrance; that way the Protestants could walk around it and the Catholics could walk over it.

Parties

Although the Irish don't generally like to drink at home (or, at least, not nearly as much as they would in a pub), there's an Irish tradition of inviting people to your house after the pub has closed for a party, or what is still sometimes known as a *hooley*. You might buy a takeaway drink from the pub before you leave, unless it's a prearranged house party, in which case somebody might have thought to organise an *iron lung* (a keg of beer) so pints could be *pulled* on tap like in a pub.

Now, get one thing very clear: the Irish quickly tire of artificial entertainment like recorded music, and no big get-together is complete until it's morphed into a *sing-song* or a dance (though the latter is less likely these days). In fact, if it's an Irish wedding, an important birthday or even a funeral, people will feel *ripped off* (cheated) without live music. Everybody's expected to contribute, so it's important that you have a *party piece* or two, most usually a song. Bear in mind that there'll be strong competition for Frank Sinatra tracks though – Old Blue Eyes' songs seem to suit the mood of the Irish *sing-song* admirably.

Young children woken up by the *rira* or *ruaille-buaille* (fun and commotion, pronounced *ruh*·la *buh*·la) might come downstairs and join the *shindig* for a short while – and even take their turn to perform a song to the delight of all the *aul' ones* (adult women in particular). Somewhere during the *wee small hours* when the hosts would like their house back, they might set the guests on their way by saying, *Time yis were spittin' in yer own ashes*. Though the last guest to depart might protest *I'll never leave until they take me out in a box*.

Traditional Irish music

Traditional Irish music and *Irish folk music* are one and the same thing and largely distinguished from other musical styles by the use of the following instruments: the *uilleann pipes* (Irish bagpipes, pronounced *il·*in), the *fiddle* (violin), the flute, the mandolin, the *bodhrán* (a type of drum, pronounced *bow·*rawn) and the accordion. The form of *traditional Irish music* around today goes back to the 18th century and possibly earlier. Amazingly enough, *traditional Irish music* is more popular now than it was a century ago, partly because back then it was being suppressed by the occupying British. At the beginning of the 20th century the *Gaelic League* emerged to revive all things Irish and began sponsoring *ceilis* (dances – pronounced *kay·*lees). Before this resurgence, *traditional Irish music* had mostly been performed solo and in instrumental *sessions* only.

The genre was given added vitality in the 1960s, when, inspired by the American folk music movement, a number of Irish groups emerged with new versions of the indigenous sounds. It was during this time that the likes of *The Clancy Brothers* and *The Dubliners* established an international audience for identifiably Irish music. Other great bands to take up the baton were *The Chieftains*, *Planxty* and *The Bothy Band* or the inimitable *Christy Moore* and *Donal Lunny*. Below are some terms associated with vernacular music:

bodhrán   a shallow one-sided drum like a large tambourine (without the metal discs), played with a double-headed beater or hit with the hand

diddle   to make traditional *mouth music* (songs with nonsense words delivered rhythmically to mimic instruments)

deedle-di-dee; *diddleeidie*; *diddly-I* phrases used to condescendingly describe *traditional Irish music*, usually by people who think it's overly sentimental and *Oirish*. You might hear something along the lines of: *Were they playing rock and roll last night, or was it diddleeidie?*

uilleann pipes Irish pipes, the sound of which was famously used in the film *Braveheart* when Scottish Highland Pipes appeared on screen, as Mel Gibson apparently preferred the sound of the Irish instrument

On the back of the renaissance of traditional Irish music, groups and musicians including ***Horslips***, ***Van Morrison*** and even ***Thin Lizzy*** were incorporating elements of traditional music into a rock idiom to form a unique new sound called, rather unfortunately, ***Celtic Rock***. This genre is alive and well today with the likes of ***U2***, ***Clannad***, ***The Cranberries***, ***The Corrs***, ***Van Morrison***, ***Sinéad O'Connor*** and ***The Pogues*** all incorporating strands of traditional music in their work, to greater or lesser degrees. Contemporary groups sticking to a more traditional bent include ***Altan***, ***Gaelic Storm***, ***Lúnasa*** and ***Solas***. Others bands such as ***Afro Celt Sound System*** and the Canadian ***Loreena McKennitt*** have adopted a multicultural fusion of styles. And love her or loathe her, ***Enya*** created a sound all her own, inspired by traditional airs, and is Ireland's bestselling solo musician ever.

Ireland has also done well in the Eurovision Song Contest, being the most successful country in the history of the competition with seven wins – a fact which fills the Irish with equal measures of pride and embarrassment.

THE SESSION

Irish traditional music ***sessions*** (***seisiún*** in Irish, pronounced *se·*shoon) are informal gatherings at which people play or sing ***traditional Irish music***. The general ***session*** format is that someone starts a tune and those who know it join in. ***Sessions*** are often held in pubs (with the hope that listeners will buy drinks for the musicians) and everyone who's able to play Irish music is welcomed usually with the words ***grab your instrument and join in***, on the assumption that they can at least hold a tune. A pub owner might have one or two musicians paid to come regularly in order for the ***session*** to have a base.

The *sessions* are a key aspect of traditional music: some say it's the main sphere in which the music is formulated and innovated. Further, the *sessions* enable young musicians to practice in a group. Socially, *sessions* have often been compared to an evening of playing card games, where the conversation and camaraderie are an essential component. In many rural communities in Ireland, *sessions* are an integral part of community life. They're an excellent way of witnessing the real, fluid identity of Irish traditional tunes. A *session* can also be called a *ceilí* (pronounced *kay·*lee) but that would more correctly include Irish dancing.

THE REBEL SONG

A subgenre of traditional Irish music, the *rebel song* is a song commemorating Ireland's desperate struggle under the *Brits* (the British). *Rebel songs* use much the same instrumentation as traditional Irish music but the lyrics are about the fight for Irish freedom, about people who were involved in liberation movements, attacks on English invaders and calls for Celtic unity. There are a number of Irish bands that specialise in the genre, including the fiery *Wolfe Tones*, and, more recently, *Eire Og*, *Athenry* and *Shebeen* from Glasgow, Scotland.

A good *rebel song* will set the scene by recounting the despicable deeds of some cowardly English person towards hard-working Irish peasants. It then moves on to the gripping details of his murder by an enraged Irishman and finishes with the rousing speech the guilty Irish patriot made from the dock before being led off by the *redcoats* (British soldiers) to be executed in some suitably bloodthirsty fashion. While many rebel songs follow this formula, the term *rebel song* is also applied fairly loosely to any song that evokes sympathy for the Irish.

It's usual for the person who starts singing a *rebel song* to know only the first verse and to repeat that over and over until

POPULAR REBEL SONGS

The Ballad of James Connolly
The inspiration for this seminal song was James Connolly, one of the leaders of the armed *1916 Rising*. The *Rising* was a key event in the history of Ireland because although it failed to oust British rule, it was a significant stepping stone on the road to Irish independence. This song describes the execution of Connolly and traces the events in the Republican struggle since that time. It's most famously sung by the Irish rebel music band the *Wolfe Tones*.

Come Out Ye Black 'n' Tans
A popular *rebel song* written by songwriter, poet, novelist and playwright Dominic Behan as a tribute to his father Stephen. The *Black and Tans* was an auxiliary paramilitary force used by the British to defend the Crown in the *War of Independence* in the 1920s. The song curses them roundly and includes many references to the struggle for Irish independence.

Fields of Athenry
One of the most famous and well-loved of all *rebel songs*, *Fields of Athenry* was penned by the prolific Irish songwriter Pete St. John in the 1970s. It relates the story of a fictional family rent apart during the *Potato Famine* of the 1840s because the British Crown transported the husband to Australia for stealing corn to feed his starving family. Because of its splendid sing-along-ability, *Fields of Athenry* has been appropriated by any gathering tinged with green.

A Nation Once Again
This classic *rebel song* was written sometime during the 1840s by Thomas Osbourn Davis (the founder of a movement for Irish independence) but has been covered countless times since – most notably by the legendary *Dubliners* and the *Wolfe Tones*. It's less vitriolic than many rebel songs but exhorts Irish men and women to stand up and fight for their land.

he or she collapses with drink or somebody takes pity on the audience and sings the whole song through, bringing it to a merciful end. It's also *de rigueur* for the singers to close their eyes, grimace and shake their head throughout for added poignancy. And when some lines are just too painful to recite (ie you've forgotten the words) just hold the tune and use nonsense lyrics along the lines of *min-na-naa-ni-na* and so forth. As well as *rebel songs* there are also a whole raft of songs in a plaintive vein that tell tales of homesickness, lost love and being far away in *Amerikay* (this is how rural Irish people used to pronounce 'America'). These are just traditional Irish songs with no rebel qualifications needed.

FAMOUS IRISH SONGS

Danny Boy
Not, as is often thought, a *rebel song*, but a love song written in 1910 by English lawyer Frederick Weatherly. Despite its foreign origins – which you'd be wise not to mention – the song has become an Irish anthem.

Dirty Old Town
Actually written about Salford in the UK by Englishman Ewan McColl, but heartily adopted by *Dubs* (Dubliners). The song was further popularised by legendary Celtic punk band The Pogues. The slurred delivery of toothless frontman, Shane MacGowan, somehow imbued the song with an added poignancy.

Green Fields of France
The Irish name for the song *No Man's Land,* written by Scottish-born Australian Eric Bogle. It commemorates slain WWI soldier Willie McBride in a rousing and heart-rending anti-war song. >

Molly Malone
This unofficial anthem of Dublin is about the beautiful (probably) fictional 17th-century fishmonger who plied her wares on the streets of Dublin crying 'Cockles and mussels, alive-alive-oh!' but died tragically of a fever. Also sung as the anthem of the Irish international rugby team.

Rare Oul' Times
Another song by Pete St John, this is a rose-tinted look back at old Dublin when everyone was poor but people were still apparently much happier than they are today.

Ride On
The title track from a well-loved album by one of Ireland's greatest ever folk singers, Christy Moore. Many of his evocative songs commemorate the deeds of individuals in Irish political struggles.

Whiskey in the Jar
A very famous song that probably dates from the 18th century and features a highwayman in the Cork and Kerry mountains who's betrayed by a woman named Jenny. It's been covered by all and sundry but nobody did a better job than the great Phil Lynott and Thin Lizzy.

Irish dancing

Ireland is rich in literature that understands a soul's yearnings, and dancing that understands a happy heart.
—Margaret Jackson

You may already have an idea of traditional Irish dance from the pulsating phenomenon of *Riverdance* or one of its clones, which, if they haven't already been to a city near you, are on their way. *Riverdance* high-kicked its way into the spotlight in 1994, when it was developed as an act to entertain the audience during an interval in the Eurovision Song Contest being hosted in Dublin that year. It took some licence with traditional dance forms but did remain broadly true to them. The traditional dance forms that it drew upon were kept alive through much of the 20th century by members of the Irish diaspora, who sought to maintain the culture of the Old Country.

Irish dancing includes solo and group forms. The solo repertoire includes the basic *jig*, *reel* and *hornpipe* tempos that can be used for various specialist dances. Group dancing is a fundamentally social activity. The ***barn dance***, for example, features people of all ages instructed by a ***caller***, and can include formations of anything from two to 16 dancers.

The classic Irish dancing costumes are based on the ***national costumes*** designed after the foundation of the ***Gaelic League*** in 1893 (an organisation which sought to preserve Irish culture). The women traditionally wear a ***brat*** (cloak) pinned at the shoulders by ***tara brooches*** (brooches featuring an ancient Celtic symbol) over a simply embroidered dress. Men traditionally wear a kilt, jacket and a cloak. Since the advent of *Riverdance*, however, the women's costumes have become altogether more elaborate while the men have been stripped back to a shirt and trousers. Another key difference between the traditional form and the contemporary twist – best exemplified by the likes of ***Michael Flatley*** (producer and director of the Lord of the Dance extravaganza) – is that men no longer have their hands practically stapled to their hips.

Oddly enough, the word *Riverdance* is also used colloquially to mean the act of committing suicide in the Shannon, Ireland's longest river, as in *So-and-so did the Riverdance*.

Other entertainment

As well as traditional music *sessions*, Ireland has all the usual outlets for musical entertainment, and you'll need no special language to access them – just a bit of charm to get past the *door bitch* (the person who sells the tickets) and/or the right clothes to impress the bouncers. There are gigs aplenty to choose from, after which you might go clubbing. Some larger pubs in cities double as dance bars or *pre-clubbing* venues where punters go to launch themselves into the night. (Preening yourself in front of the mirror before a *night on the razzle*, by the way, is called getting yourself *done up* for a big night out.)

Temple Bar in Dublin is a favourite haunt for *stag parties* (a fiancé's last hurrah before the wedding), and *hen parties* (the female equivalent) and for groups of overseas tourists. You can see many *unfortunates* there at weekends, often in their underwear after a big night. It's in an area near the quays, and although it's home to some cool places like the U2-owned Clarence Hotel, locals generally avoid the bar and call it *Temple Barf* after all the *pissheads* it attracts.

Shopping

It's only quite recently, since the *Celtic Tiger* (Irish economy) delivered heavier wallets and plumper purses, that shopping has become more than a chore for the Irish (although they themselves would never admit that). Now it's a major social activity to which they devote plenty of time, effort and money.

On Saturday afternoons, towns and cities all over Ireland are *dubh la daoine* with people out shopping (an Irish phrase meaning literally 'black with people', pronounced duv le dee·nee). *High streets* (the main street of a town), with strips of popular stores, are common, while more and more *dear* (expensive) boutique stores are opening up and becoming destinations in their own right. And, of course, if you're short on time or patience, there are also plenty of department stores and US-style shopping malls springing up in the suburbs.

Along with tonnes of tourist tack, such as factory-made *hawthorn sticks* (powerful wands according to Irish folklore) and anything you can put a *shamrock* on, there's also a burgeoning industry of contemporary products from new designers. If that doesn't *ring your bell*, you can always rely on traditional wares like *Waterford Crystal*, *Aran sweaters*, *Irish tweed* or *linen* and handcrafted *Celtic jewellery*. Northern Ireland is also home to the exquisite *Belleek*, *Tara* and *Irish Dresden* ceramics. A *Cashback* sticker displayed in shops means that non-EU residents can get a *VAT* (Value Added Tax – the Irish sales tax) refund on the goods they buy when they leave Ireland. If you're out shopping you might come across the following consumerist terminology too:

getting something on the never-never or *on the drip* (buying something on hire purchase)

getting the messages (this expression means 'going grocery shopping')

guaranteed Irish (no cheap imitation foreign stuff)

Don't be surprised if, when you walk into a shop, the attendant asks *Are you're all right?* In this case it just means 'Would you like help with anything?' On the other side of the counter you might hear a shopper saying something like *Give us (a Mars Bar)*. It's a curiosity but Irish shoppers often replace 'I' with 'us' when asking for something in a shop. And perhaps it's just part of making conversation, but it's often insufficient for Irish shoppers just to ask for something, they also explain why they want it. They might buy *spuds for the dinner* or *shoes for the cousin's wedding*, for example.

Movies, theatre & TV

MOVIES

Going to the *flicks*, the *pictures* – or, if you're over 65, the *picture house* – to watch a film (pronounced 'filuhm') is, of course, widely popular and the perfect tonic on a miserable wet Irish day. A common question is *Was the film any use?* (pronounced like the verb 'use') meaning 'Was the film any good?' If you liked it, it was *the business*, if not, it was *shite*. *All right* would suggest it was neither here nor there.

The Irish film industry has grown rapidly in recent years, thanks largely to its promotion by *Bord Scannán na hÉireann* (The Irish Film Board, pronounced bord *sko*·nawn na *hay*·rin) and the introduction of heavy tax breaks. Today more and more films are being produced in Ireland and many of these films and Irish actors and directors have won international acclaim and awards. Some of the hit films of the last decades include: *Angela's Ashes, The Butcher Boy, The Commitments, The General, In the Name of the Father, I Went Down, Michael Collins, My Left Foot, The Snapper, The Van* and *Waking Ned Devine*.

IRISH STARS OF THE SCREEN

For a small country, Ireland has produced far more movie stars than by rights it should have. Here are a few of our *faves* (favourites).

Kenneth Branagh
Belfast-born and English-raised Branagh made his name with film adaptations of Shakespeare, and earned the respect of the Irish for turning down a knighthood.

Daniel Day-Lewis
One of the most dedicated and gifted actors of his generation, Day-Lewis has made some terrific films – his portrayal of Christy Brown in *My Left Foot* will be hard to beat.

Colin Farrell

Pseudo-working-class *Dub* (Dubliner) Colin Farrell has been the Hollywood 'it boy' for the last few years and is most famous for trying to shag anything with a pulse.

Brenda Fricker

The first lady of Irish film (actually one of the *only* prominent ladies of Irish film), Fricker won an Oscar for best supporting actress playing Christy Brown's mum in *My Left Foot*. Fricker's name in the credits usually guarantees a decent flick.

Colm Meaney

The Dublin actor who attained immortality as the father in *The Snapper* based on Roddy Doyle's book. He went on to make a few bob as Miles O'Brien in *Star Trek* but has so far failed to realise his full potential.

Liam Neeson

A former youth boxing champion, Northern Irish Neeson combines brain and brawn and has made some outstanding features, including *Schindler's List*, for which he won an Oscar.

Peter O'Toole

Hailing from Connemara in Galway, the debonair and charismatic O'Toole is most famous for his role in *Lawrence of Arabia* and won the Academy Honorary Award for his lifelong contribution to film in 2003. Still making movies well into his 70s.

Stephen Rea

Belfast-born and working class, Rea is one of the most successful and highly respected stay-at-home actors in the country and is most famous for his leading role in Neil Jordan's film *The Crying Game*. Although he's a Protestant, Rea is a staunch Republican and is married to a former IRA hunger-striker.

THEATRE

All the world's a stage and most of us are desperately unrehearsed.
—Sean O'Casey

Irish theatre has enjoyed world renown for centuries, although it's rarely mentioned that it was those dastardly English occupiers who set it up in the first place – in the 17th century to be precise. Since then, as with many cultural pursuits, the Irish have made a disproportionate contribution to world drama.

The 20th century was the golden age for Irish theatre, due in no small measure to the establishment of the famed Abbey Theatre in Dublin in 1899. Luminaries such as JM Synge, Sean O'Casey and WB Yeats had their plays first performed there and largely shaped what's regarded today as *classic Irish theatre*. The Abbey Theatre has traditionally had a strong focus on presenting plays that bring different dialects of Irish English to the stage.

Many other Irish playwrights rose to prominence later in the 20th century, including Samuel Beckett and Brendan Behan, and later Tom Murphy, Hugh Leonard and John B Keane. Irish theatre is still in great nick today, shaping the hugely successful careers of people like Roddy Doyle, Brian Friel and Peter Sheridan.

TELEVISION

Although Ireland punches well above its weight in cinema and theatre, it's a puny and underperforming featherweight when it comes to television. A couple of hours watching *the box*, *telly* or *goggle box* could well blow the country's reputation for being on the cultural cutting edge. As the Irish themselves would say, most of their terrestrial television is *shite*. Irish viewers might well have gone bonkers over the years if they hadn't been able to switch *sides* (channels) to British stuff and sign up for *piped TV* (cable television) which has been taken up with alacrity. That said, it's worth tuning in to the news just to hear the famous plummy accent on *Dublin 4* of *RTÉ1* and the Irish-language channel *TG4* to hear Irish.

TV HOUSEHOLD NAMES

Anne Doyle
Presents the main evening news on the national broadcaster *RTÉ*. She stepped into the world of television from the Irish Department of Foreign Affairs and had a well-publicised relationship with a former government minister.

Gaybo
Gabriel 'Gay' Byrne (nicknamed Gaybo), universally-loved long-time host of *The Late Late Show*, Ireland's answer to *The Tonight Show* (from which he retired in 1999), and a host of other TV series. Though officially retired, he resurfaces to host the odd TV series and on the radio.

Eddie Hobbs
A financial adviser who does a show on TV called *Rip Off Ireland*, bringing the nation's attention to the exorbitant prices of everyday goods.

Pat Kenny
Host of the *The Late Late Show*, and a fairly wooden character in comparison to Gerry Ryan. Unkindly dubbed *Pat the Plank* by well-known critic and shit-stirrer Eamon Dunphy.

Miriam O'Callaghan
A current affairs broadcaster on *RTÉ* and presenter of the show *Prime Time*. She also heads a documentary film production company, Mint Productions, which most notably produced a documentary called the *Outsider* about the maverick former Prime Minister Charles Haughey.

Gerry Ryan
An institution both loved and loathed on Irish TV and radio. His long-running *The Gerry Ryan Show* is Ireland's most popular radio programme. He's Ireland's number one shock jock, and his non-stop banter frequently causes outrage.

Television has left its mark on Irish popular culture in the form of the following catchphrases:

Get up the yard   meaning 'get out of it/you're having me on/what do you take me for?' The *yard* most likely refers to the yardarm of a sailing ship. For true Dubliners the term is followed by ***There's a smell of Benjy (Riordan) off ya***; Benjy Riordan being the clichéd *culchie* (country bumpkin) from *The Riordans*, a soap opera about life in a rural Irish village, which was the most successful serial in the history of *RTÉ*, and ran for 15 years.

Stop the lights!   comes from the 1960s *RTÉ* quiz show *Quicksilver*. In order to pass on a question, a contestant would have to call this phrase out, and it became a response to any question that a person could not, or did not, want to answer. Now it's used to mean 'Stop doing that' or as an exclamation of surprise (equivalent to 'Really?' or 'Good grief!').

Gambling

A more dubious form of entertainment – albeit one that's very popular in Ireland, at least when it comes to horse racing and sport – gambling is a favourite pastime for the Irish. You can find *bookies* (bookmakers) on every *high street* and beside many pubs.

There isn't really a casino culture – what are commonly called casinos in Ireland are places with lots of sound effects, flashing lights and games like video poker and slot machines. The wagers are low and the atmosphere titanium-strength tacky. Much more popular is the *lotto* (the national lottery), more commonly referred to as the *bleedin' lotto* because people get hooked, get their hopes up and, of course, usually don't win. *Scratchies* (scratch lottery cards) are also big.

Festivals & get-togethers

The Irish need no excuse to kick up their heels and have a plethora of festivals of various sizes celebrating all sorts of things including music, sport, history, art, food and even knitting.

Music fans are spoilt for choice, with major venues such as *Slane Castle* and the *Point Depot* in Dublin and the *Odyssey* and the *Waterfront Hall* in Belfast regularly showcasing the best of Irish and international musical talent.

Literature buffs enjoy the literary festivals and summer schools, including the *Yeats Winter and Summer School* held in Sligo in February and August, *Listowel Writers Week* held in County Kerry in June and the *Bard of Armagh Festival of Humorous Verse* which takes place in June. Film fans can savour international film festivals in Belfast, Cork, Galway, Derry and Dublin.

There's also a wide range of fairly highbrow festivals such as the *Galway Arts Festival* in July, which attracts the world's best writers and performers. The *Kilkenny Arts Festival* in August draws an exciting mix of visitors from around Ireland and abroad. The *Belfast Festival* at Queens takes place every autumn and brings together the very best of international talent and the *Dublin Theatre Festival* plays host to an eclectic mix of the world's finest productions.

For the palate, Ireland has many festivals and events throughout the year, including the *Galway Oyster Festival* and the *World Oyster Eating Championships* at Hillsborough, both in September. The following month in Kinsale (supposedly the Gourmet Capital of Ireland) there's the *Autumn Flavours Festival of Fine Food and Fun*. On a slightly smaller scale, local fairs, where people come to sell their wares, listen to music and socialise, take place all over Ireland.

Even affairs of the heart are catered for: if you've come to Ireland looking for true love, amble down to the (admittedly very corny and conservative) *Lisdoonvarna Matchmaking Festival* which takes place every year in September.

Below, are a sample of some other festivals and fairs held annually throughout the country.

MUSIC

Cork International Choral Festival held in April/May, this is one of the big ones for the choral community

Fleadh Cheoil na hÉireann held in a different town every August, this is the most important of all the traditional music festivals

Music Festival in Great Irish Houses held during June, this festival involves classical music concerts at stately homes around the country

Willie Clancy Summer School one of the biggest traditional music events of the year takes place in Miltown Malbay, County Clare, in July

SPORT

All Ireland Hurling and Football Finals Dublin hosts the biggest sporting events of the year, separated by a fortnight in September

Galway Races a week-long horse racing festival held at Ballybrit Racecourse in Galway during July/August, the main events of which are the ***Galway Plate*** and the ***Galway Hurdle***

Irish Derby Stakes a popular thoroughbred horse racing meet, held in June at the Curragh Racecourse in Kildare. The Stakes attract the best three-year-old colts and fillies from Great Britain and the Continent.

Irish Grand National a large horse racing event held in April at Fairyhouse in County Meath. Run over a three-mile course, it's Ireland's richest and most prestigious ***steeplechase*** event.

MISCELLANEOUS FESTIVALS

The Cat Laughs Festival an outstanding comedy festival held in June each year and featuring the cream of Irish comedy (of which there is much), as well as some big names from the international stage

Derry Halloween Carnival features street theatre, music and mayhem, especially during the fireworks display on October 31

Oul' Lammas Fair four hundred years old and still going strong, this traditional market fair in Ballycastle in August is a major crowd-puller, with music, dancing, sport and entertainment

Puck Fair one of Ireland's oldest festivals is a traditional horse fair, which includes open-air concerts and a fireworks display, in Killorglin, County Kerry, during August

Rose of Tralee International Festival a big international event held in County Kerry every August and centring on a contest to find the Irish woman who personifies the best of Ireland in looks and personality

St Patrick's Day there are celebrations all over Ireland on March 17, including a national festival in Dublin and major events in all the larger towns and cities

You could say that the Irish love the sound of their own voices, as they take genuine delight in the way words sound as much as in their meaning. Nowhere is this more evident than in slang expressions – or as the Irish would say, the *local lingo* – used in everyday conversations with friends and family. While much of this colourful language might seem impenetrable to an outsider, the aim isn't to be exclusive: the Irish just like playing with their words. Most of these phrases are peculiar to Ireland and those that seem familiar may have taken on particular nuances and subtleties since being absorbed into the Irish vernacular.

Doing things

blagged someone ourra it	to have got the better of someone
blem	to kick
bobble	to walk or move somewhere
burst	to beat (someone) up
Calm your jets!	Don't stress! Take it easy!
clock a girl	pick up a girl; see a girl you fancy
dialled	to be finished, understood or sorted
faffin'; faffin' about	to dawdle or fuss
fooster	to dilly-dally
gaiging; geigin	a term used by the *travelling* community to describe public begging

gawk	to stare
give out	to complain – the nation will *give out* about their soccer team's poor performance, for example
gumming for it	to be eager or to yearn for something; a similar expression is *There's a smell of want off ye*
lamp	depending where you are in Ireland it can mean 'to punch' (Dublin, Belfast) or 'to look' (Cork)
lash	to try or attempt as in *I'll give it a lash*
lash into	more often that not it means a severe telling-off rather than a physical altercation
lay into	to give someone a beating
loaf	to head-butt someone
lose one's Paddy	to throw a tantrum, also *throw a Paddy*
mollycoddle	to be overprotective
mooch	to try and seduce a woman – common in the phrase *on the mooch*
mugging the head	kissing – as in *I was mugging the head off of him*
peg it	to make a hasty getaway
poxed	to be very worn out
pull a tom and dick	to go home sick
put the mockers on	to put a hex on or jinx something
scarper; skedaddle	to make a quick getaway
slinjing	dragging your feet – as in kids going to school *slinjing* all the way
spot	to lend – as in *can you spot me a pound for a jar* (a drink)?
Stall the ball!	Wait a moment!
suckin' diesel	to be having a good time

People

THIN

If someone has a thin face you could say about them that *they could kiss a goat between its horns*. If there's a thin person that annoys you, you can dismiss them as *a lanky streak of piss*. A childish word for 'thin' is *skinnymalink*, which is sometimes incorporated into schoolyard taunts such as *skinnymalink melodeon legs* (pronounced 'mulogeon legs') or *skinnymalink umbrella feet* (pronounced 'umberella fee'). Other expressions to describe emaciated types:

if she turned sideways you'd miss her
more meat on a jockey's whip
not a pick on 'im
you'd lose her in the long grass

STATURE OR BUILD

If you're talking about build or stature you can't go past the distinctively Irish description of a short person as *not tall enough to pick a shamrock* or the humorous *he has a straight back on him like he just swallowed a crowbar*. However, here are a few others:

beef on the heel like a Mullingar heifer	a big woman
the big wind wouldn't stir him/her	he or she is big

butty	an adjective used to describe a girl or woman who's neither tall nor fat, but has a certain girth
horse box	a stocky bloke
like a farmer	generally someone with broad shoulders
mountainy	denotes someone big and rough
a neck like a bull	a fat-necked individual
puchan	(pronounced *pukh*·an) a girl or woman of below-average height – derived from the Irish for 'young goat'

OLD/SICK/OUT OF SORTS

Hungover individuals might be accused of having eyes looking *like pissholes in the snow* or of *looking like a shit after a shower*. If someone's just being *a right misery guts* you can describe their depressed state of mind (and appearance) thus:

goin' around like a constipated greyhound
he's a face on him as long as today and tomorra
she's a face on her as long as a hare's back leg
he'd walk across a field and never see a daisy
moping around like a straying ass

For other ailments the following descriptors might apply:

blind in one eye and can't see with the other
he has this aul' back what follies him around (said of a
    person suffering from a bad back – *follies* means follows)
my head's splittin'/opening (I've got a headache)
old for his age
the flesh just walked off him lately

UNKEMPT/BAD TEMPERED

There are some colourful ways to describe facial expressions. Someone who's looking angry can have *a face that would box a goat*. About a sour-looking person you could say *if she died with that face, nobody would wash her* or you could say that she has *a face like a Lurgan spade* (*Lurgan* is an anglicisation of the Irish word for a spade with a long blade used for cutting peat). People of rough appearance get the following treatment:

she has hair on her like rats' tails
he's crawling with fleas (often shortened to just **he's crawling**)
like something that fell off a tinker's cart and wasn't missed

PERSONALITY

There's no shortage of creative Irish vocabulary when it comes to describing personalities. Someone who drives you mad is a **wreck-the-head**, **lob-sided pox bottle** or **sap**; a boring person is dismissed as a **big long drink of water** or a **dry shite**. A character who looks good on the outside but who underneath is a lightweight is described as a **fur coat and no knickers**. Almost the full gamut of personality types is dissected in the gallery of expressions below:

arse licker; **gicker**	someone fond of sucking up
aul' biddy	an annoying old woman
blackguard; **blaggard**	originally 'an annoying person' but often used now as a term of endearment for a mischievous person
bockedy-arsed aul' bitch	an uncomplimentary way of referring to a woman (the word **bockedy** means 'bent or crooked')
cannat	a mischievous, provocative person
chancer	a dodgy character who constantly tries his luck
dog wide	someone who doesn't miss a trick

dosser	a layabout
hatstand	a peculiar person
hoor's melt	someone you hate
jibber	someone who's afraid to try new things
laudydaw; Lord Muck	a stuck-up or posh person who gives themselves airs
me aul' segotia/ sweat/flower	your best friend (used by older people)
melter	a person with very annoying tendencies
poxy	lousy
a right clippin' of tin	a troublemaker
scully	a prankster – also used as a verb to mean 'being up to no good'
spoofer	someone who tells lies and is generally untrustworthy
toaster	someone who's a bit odd
woolly	an adjective to describe someone who's confused

These phrases describe various personality traits:

a bigger bollocks never put his arm through a coat a dismissive comment about someone you don't like

afraid to sneeze in case he'd give something away tight-fisted

can't see beyond his nose self-centred

fit to mind mice at a cross-roads a worthless person

gas craic, altogether very entertaining, a laugh-and-a-half – (*gas* means 'funny' and *craic* means 'fun')

has an eye like a stinkin' eel someone who watches every-thing *has a neck like a jockey's bollocks* or *has some neck on him/ her* a very cheeky person

if bullshit was music, that fella'd be a brass band a teller of tall tales, especially about himself

if he went any slower he'd catch up with himself on the way back someone who's slow

she'd spend everything and what she's not given she'll take a greedy person

she'd talk the cross off an ass's back/the teeth off a saw a very talkative person

she'd make you die laughing a very funny person

she has an eye that would see round corners a very observant person

he says more than his prayers a talkative person, most of whose prattle is not to be trusted

a street angel and a house devil someone who's well-behaved in public but a nightmare at home

that fellow'll be late for his own funeral a person who is unpunctual

he thinks he's the cat's pyjamas thinks he's perfect

yer man would be a good messenger to send for Death said of someone who's slow in doing things

NOT ALL THERE
A person who's a bit of an idiot or stupid or crazy might be referred to as *one of God's children*. Other less charitable expressions to describe such people include:

a couple of sandwiches short of a picnic
a couple of spanners short of a tool box
he hasn't the brains of a sparrow
if brains were cotton wool, he wouldn't have enough to make a tampon for a budgie

Ignorant people, meanwhile, get short shrift in the following terms:

he doesn't know his head from his arse or his arse from his elbow
she knows no more about it than a pig does about an armchair

Actions

blackguarding	(pronounced 'blaggarding') what someone's doing when they're annoying you
do it fairly lively	accomplish something quickly
has my heart crucified	causes me immense heartache
putting it on the long finger/ back burner	to procrastinate
the road	the way to do something – as in *I wasn't able to plaster until Da showed me the road to do it*
shenanigans	intrigue, trickery or manoeuvres designed to effect a certain outcome

And a few more expressions:

she filled your head full of white mice   someone lied to you or made big promises but didn't deliver on them

I believe you when hundreds wouldn't   what you're saying sounds a bit far-fetched but I'll give you the benefit of the doubt

you couldn't hit a cow's arse with a banjo you have a bad aim (eg a woeful *hurler*, darts or soccer player)

whatever you say, say nothing don't say anything about it

you're like a pig knitting you're useless (at something) – might be said when you have a bad driver in front of you

Situations

In an embarrassing situation there's a host of expressions to describe your humiliation. You could say *I was stung, I was scarlet, I got a reddner, I didn't know where to put my face* or *I was morto* (mortified). In the North the words of choice to describe embarrassment are *scundered* or *affronted*. Here are some other terms to describe everyday situations:

Any odds?	(or *gis yer odds*) have you got spare change?
Are you right?	what somebody will keep repeating when they're waiting impatiently for you
boss	a term of deference, especially when proffering an item or service for sale, as in *Arya alright there boss?*
holy terror	chaotic – as in *the traffic was a holy terror*; or a description of a mischeivous child
laid out like an altar	a well-dressed person
like a wet night in Athlone	a boring occasion that seemed to go on and on
Whisht!	Hush!

hasn't as much on her as would keep flies off a sugar bowl a scantily dressed girl

I didn't know whether to shite or get a haircut! very excited about something

I wouldn't do that for man nor beast I wouldn't do it under any circumstances *starvin' the mice out of their holes*   said of a host whose portions of food are considered inadequate. If they have the temerity to offer you a particularly small draft of whiskey, you could assert *Ah jaysus, ya wouldn't fill your tooth with that!*

Colloquial expressions

The Irish can be pretty direct in everyday conversation. One characteristic retort meaning 'there's no way I'll do that' is *I will in me bollix!* which has the equally colourful variants *I will in me gee*, *I will in me hole* and *I will in me ring!* If Irish people want to swear that they're telling the truth, they might use the expressions *God's honest truth*, *not a word of a lie* or *on me mother's life*.

If someone comes up with a particularly surprising piece of information, it might be met with the exclamation *that beats Banagher* (that's the best I've heard yet). Banagher in Offaly was a *rotten* (corrupt) borough in the old Irish parliament – political contests were rare in Offaly, the MP usually being the person nominated by the local landlord or whoever else 'owned' the seat. Here are a few more exclamations and declamations.

Dry up!	Shut up!
Dry yer eyes!	Stop crying (or whinging)! – particularly used in the North
Get on side!	Behave yourself!
Get out o' that garden!	Get lost, you liar!
Give my head peace!	Stop nagging or annoying me!
I am in me wick!	You must be joking!
If I were mad, I would!	No way!
I see, says the blind man!	said when the penny drops and you finally grasp some concept

I will so!	I certainly will! (said with an indignant tone)
Keep your breath to cool your porridge!	You can stop talking now, you're wasting your time.
Luvly hurdlin'!	That's a great job!
Not too shabby	pretty good
Pull your socks up!	Get to work!
Would you ever go 'n' cultivate yourself!	Go and get yourself some manners!
You have your glue!	Don't be silly!
You're like the police.	You're never where you're wanted.

Humorous sayings

No one can dispute that the Irish have a well-developed sense of humour and enjoy a bit of wordplay. Here's a selection of creative language with a humorous bent:

definitely probably a common qualifier (after all, the Irish don't want to be wrong)

he's a dog that can have pups used by someone who'd prefer to avoid the word 'bitch' when referring to a female dog

he's very handy with his feet said about a dancer or footballer

let the dog see the rabbit show it to me then I'll understand it – used when someone's describing an object that the listener can't see

that's wettin' rain meaning it'll stop you from doing what you want to do, as opposed to the nearly constant drizzle *the song the oul' cow died to*   a description of a piece of music which doesn't appeal to the listener

Whatya hopin' for, a boy or a child?   jokingly said to an expectant father

The Irish also have a bit of a knack with funny one-liners:

How I wish Adam had died with all his ribs in his body   a man might say this when the women are picking on him

Jaysus, I'd forget me balls if they weren't in a sack   an admission of absent-mindedness

IRISH WITTICISMS

Among English-speakers, the Irish are the undisputed masters of wit. They have an uncanny knack for coining humourous sayings imbued with a good dose of insight and common sense. Irish writers are renowned especially; none more so than the incomparable Oscar Wilde. The quips below (though not penned by Wilde) could put a smile on your face *as broad as the Shannon* (Ireland's longest river).

An Englishman thinks he's being moral when he's only being uncomfortable.

An Irish atheist is one who wishes to God he could believe in Him.

An Irish politician is a man of few words, but he uses them often.

An Irish queer is a fellow who prefers women to drink.

Anyone who's not confused in Northern Ireland doesn't know what's going on.

Have you heard about the Irish boomerang? It doesn't come back; it just sings sad songs about how much it wants to.

'As ... as a'

The comparative expression *as ... as a* yields a world of possibilities in Irish slang. If someone's poured a cup of very weak tea (a cardinal sin, as the Irish like their tea full-bodied) it can be disparagingly described as *as weak as an infant child*. What might elsewhere be described as 'as scarce as hen's teeth' is given a creative twist as well in the expression *as scarce as rocking-horse shite*. Some other well-known comparisons follow:

as bald as a coot
as bent as a shepherd's crook
as black as twelve o'clock
as clear as ditchwater
as cross as a bag of cats
as deaf as a badger
as dry as dishwater (dry in the sense of 'humourless')
as fat as a bishop
as fat as a fool
as hardy as a mountain goat
as hoarse as a drake
as honest as the sun
as mean as cat's shite
as odd as two left feet
as rough as a bear's arse
as sick as a small hospital
as small as a mouse's diddy (*diddy* means 'breast')
as soft as shite
as sound as a pound
as thin as a whippet
as useful/useless as ...
    a bucket of steam
    a cigarette lighter on a motorbike
    a chocolate teapot
    a rubber hammer
as wild as a march hare
as wild as a mountain goat

Rhyming slang

Although rhyming slang was originally part of the Cockney dialect from the East End of London, the Irish took a shine to the form long ago and cross-fertilised it with the local vernacular. It's a slang repository that's constantly being updated as new terms are introduced and others fall out of favour.

apples and pears	stairs
apple tart	a fart
arabs knees	keys
Arthur Power	a shower
ball of chalk	a walk
ballymunner	a runner (*to do a ballymunner* means to get the hell out of somewhere)
Barney Dillons	shillings (ie money)
Barney Rubble	trouble
battle cruiser	a boozer (otherwise known as a pub)
Bill Murray	a curry
Bill Skinner	dinner
boat race	a face
bowler hat	a rat
bread and honey	money
Brenda Frickers	knickers (after the Irish actress)
brown bread	dead
bucket of dirt	shirt
bull and cow	a row (fight)
carry cots	spots
Chevy Chase	a face
chicken's neck	cheque
chicken's hash	cash
Christian Slater	later
cock and hen	ten
daisy roots	boots
Davy Crockett	a pocket
Davie Gower	a shower
Dick van Dyke	a bike

Dickie Diver	a fiver (money)
dig in the grave	a shave
dog and bone	a phone
Esther Ranzen	dancing
far east	priest
garden hose	a nose
george raft	draught (breeze)
Gregory Peck	a neck
Gregory Pecks	specs
half scotch	a watch
ham and cheesy	easy
hambone	a phone
horses and asses	glasses
house of wax	jacks
Indian Joes	toes
jam jar	car
Jimmy Joyce	voice
Joe Roofer	spoofer – someone who tells tall tales

Joe Skinner	your dinner
kangaroo	rhyme for 'thankin' you'
kitchen sink	a chink (crack)
Lee Marvin	starving
Lou Reed	speed
mince pie	an eye
MiWadi	a body (after the Irish cordial brand)
monkey's paw	a draw (on a cigarette)
Nat King	the dole (unemployment benefit)
north and south	a mouth
Oliver Twist	a wrist
ones and twos	shoes
pedal and crank	a wank
Peggy Dell	a smell
pie and trash	hash

plates of meat	feet
raspberry ripples	nipples
raspberry tart	a heart
Roger Moore	whore
Rosie Lee	tea
Scooby Doo	clue
scotch peg	leg
skyrocket	pocket
tennis racket	jacket
thruppenny bits	tits
tin of fruit	a suit
two by four	door
Uncle Ned	head
Vera Lynns	skins

Smart & cheeky answers

Even when Irish people don't know much about a subject, you'll never catch them short of an opinion on anything, and it usually comes in the form of a smart remark. Perhaps that was what Oscar Wilde was getting at in his often-quoted epigram: 'If one could only teach the English how to talk, and the Irish how to listen, society here would be quite civilised.'

When you say you don't know where something is and it's right in front of you, the Irish might tease you with *If it had a mouth it'd bite you in the arse* or *What's that, Scotch mist on a cloudy day?* A smart answer to the question *Where's so-and-so?* might be *Up me arse picking daisies* or *Up in Nellie's room behind the wallpaper* (meaning 'how the hell should I know?'). And if you ask someone where they're going and that person doesn't want to tell you, they might retort *To there and back to see how far it is* or *To see a man about a dog*.

When you ask someone about something they don't want to tell you, they might say with mock incredulity *Did I not tell you earlier?* When you answer 'no', they'll most probably say *Well it mustn't be any of your bleedin' business then.* If you're sick of someone's company, you could try asking them *Can you ride a motorbike?* If they say 'yes', your comeback is *Well rev up and fuck off!*

When you haven't seen somebody for a long time and they suddenly appear, you could say *Well the dead arose and appeared to many!* or just plain *Ah the dead arose! I don't know yez from the dogs* means 'I've never seen you before and know nothing about you'. If someone's setting off somewhere unprepared (or inappropriately dressed) you can give them a dressing down with the phrase *Where would you be going with no bell on your bike, and your knickers at half-mast?* And if someone's just dropped a bombshell, the standard expression of amazement is *Well Jesus, Mary and holy sweet Joseph, why didn't you tell me?*

Congratulating someone can be accomplished by trotting out the phrases *Well, fair play to you, anyhow!* or *Fair fucks to you!* both of which amount to a big pat on the back. And when someone's got you roundly entertained, you can encourage them with the remark *You're gas craic, your mother must have been a cylinder!* (*gas* means 'funny' and *craic* means 'good times').

Animals, pets & pests

A mongrel dog can be jokingly referred to as *half a cocker and half a conger eel*. Some other common animals have distinctive names in Irish English, many of them coming from Irish:

arcan	a small pig
banbh; **bonnam**	a pig (especially a piglet)
brock	a badger
cleg	a horsefly
clock	a large black beetle
croil	an undersized animal or dwarf (especially common in Ulster)

cur	a dog
easog	a weasel
hairy molly	the black fuzzy caterpillars of the cabbage white butterfly
kittlings	kittens
man-eater; midge; mite	a newt
ossal	a donkey (also in some parts of Ireland the standard English word is pronounced 'dunkey')
pinkeen	a minnow fish
pishmires	ants
selmide	(pronounced *shel*·mi·dah) snail
sile an phortaigh	(pronounced *shee*·la on *for*·tig) a heron
striddly	a stickleback fish

Drug culture

All the usual slang words are used for drugs (*blow*, *joint*, *spliff*, *smack* and so on) but Irish English has coined a few druggy terms of its own as well. A joint is called a *bifter*, a *jumbo* or a *marley*, and someone who's stoned is described as *cabbaged*, *mushed*, *off their tits* or *outta their box*. Read on for some more druggy terms:

disco biscuits	ecstasy tablets
don't be bogartin'	pass the joint
henry	means an 'eight' of coke (from King Henry VIII)
hot rocks	the burning bits of hash and paper that flake off from the business end of a joint
jack dee	ecstasy

Parnell	cocaine (from Ireland's most famous 'Charlie' – politician Charles Stewart Parnell)
sneachta	(the Irish word for 'snow', pronounced *snokh*·ta) cocaine
tin mugs	drugs
turf	hash – as in *You get the pipe and I'll get the turf*
turf patrol	a hashish-smoking session
winged; wired	to be high on ecstasy
yakker	someone who does hard drugs, eg a heroin junkie
yokes	ecstacy

A few Irish acronyms & terms

AIB	Allied Irish Bank
Aosdana	(pronounced *ays*·duh·na) the elite arts body
An Taisce	(pronounced on *tash*·keh) the national body monitoring heritage and the environment
Árd Fheis	(pronounced ord esh) an annual convention, usually of a political party
B of I	Bank of Ireland
Fáinne	(pronounced *fawn*·yeh) a lapel pin worn by fluent Irish-speakers
Gaeltacht	(pronounced *gayl*·takht) the areas where Irish is spoken as a first language
Gaeilge	(pronounced *gayl*·ge) the Irish name for the indigenous Irish language
IBEC	the Irish Business and Employers' Confederation – the national voice of Irish business and employers

ICTU	the Irish Congress of Trade Unions (an all-Ireland body)
IFA	the Irish Farmers Association – the main farmers' body in the Republic of Ireland
RDS	the Royal Dublin Society – originally established to promote agriculture, it stages the annual Dublin Horse Show
RnaG	Radio na Gaeltachta (pronounced *ra*·dee·o na *gayl*·takh·ta), the Irish-language radio station
SIPTU	the Services Industrial, Professional and Technical Union – the largest trade union in Ireland
SPUC	the Society for the Protection of the Unborn Child – a large anti-abortion group
Údarás na Gaeltachta	(pronounced *oo*·dar·aws na *gayl*·takh·ta) the state-sponsored body responsible for the development of industry and the language in Irish-speaking areas

MISUNDERSTANDINGS

Despite the spirit of sharing that exists between Irish English and other forms of English, there are numerous instances of disagreement over which word to use. For example, *gas* means 'funny', *craic* (pronounced 'crack') means 'a good time', *dear* is expensive, *ass* is a donkey – but *arse* is what you sit on (just in case speakers of US or Canadian English get confused). The *bog* is anywhere in Ireland outside of Dublin but the *bogs* are the toilets. Nothing gets broken if something is *smashing*, it's just 'great'. If you hear a mother berating a child for being *bold*, it means 'naughty', not 'brave'. Most things are *grand*, which has nothing to do with opulence, but is a way of saying things are 'great'. Also note that *Celtic* when used as an adjective to describe the race or culture is always pronounced with a hard *C* – 'keltik' – while any sports team with *Celtic* in its name uses the soft *C*, pronouncing the word 'seltik'. Following are some of the most common examples of potential misunderstandings.

Misconceptions

Resist the temptation to use the greeting *top of the morning*, as it's only been heard to date in corny Hollywood movies on an *Oirish* theme, such as the Fred Astaire movie *Finian's Rainbow*. Other no-no's include the exclamations *bedad* and *begorrah* (both altered versions of 'by God!'). Calling a woman *a fine colleen* (a literary or humorous term for a girl) is likely to lead to you getting a knee in the groin before her brother gives you a *clatter* (a blow) across the head. The full-blooded expression *Come on to fuck!* isn't an invitation to get intimate, but an exasperated urging to hurry up, sort yourself out, try harder or stop being so disappointingly rubbish (in a sporting sense).

In the lists below are words that could give rise to misunderstandings if Irish English speakers fraternise with either UK English or US English speakers. Speakers of other varieties of English might also be able to relate to some of the potential linguistic pitfalls involved.

UK English

Irish English	UK English	Irish English	UK English
brutal	very bad	jacks	loo
cooker	stove	kip	a dive (a seedy place)
dummy tit	baby's dummy	minerals	soft drinks
eejit	idiot	piped telly	cable TV
gas	funny	press	cupboard
grand	great	soother	baby's dummy
guard	bobby (policeman)	wojus	very bad

US English

Irish English	US English	Irish English	US English
biscuit	cookie	jacks	restroom
bogs	restroom	path	sidewalk
brolly	umbrella	pavement	a sidewalk
chemist	drugstore	pissed	drunk
chips	fries	pram	baby's pushchair
crisps	chips		
cross	to be angry	rubber	eraser
dispensary	drugstore	runners	sneakers
fag	cigarette	a shot	a chance
flat	apartment	strand	beach
go-car	baby's pushchair	tackies	sneakers
lift	a ride; an elevator	telly	TV

REGIONAL VARIATIONS

There are only two dialects of Irish, plain Irish and toothless Irish, and, lacking a proper acquaintance with the latter, I think I missed the cream of the old man's talk.
—Frank O'Connor from *Leinster, Munster and Connaught*

In spite of its small size, if you look or listen closely enough you'll soon realise that Ireland is a collection of different cities, towns, villages and distinct tribes that have grown together (and sometimes apart) over the millennia. Irish English reflects this diversity and a well-trained ear can distinguish between four or five different accents in Dublin alone and identify dozens around the country as a whole.

Rivalries between neighbouring villages and towns – usually sporting though frequently political in the North – can be fierce but the discernible differences (linguistic and otherwise) between opposing camps are relatively slight. But hang around a while and listen closely, and the local origins of speakers will soon reveal themselves.

Geographical realities

Before we take a peek at dialect diversity in Irish English, it makes sense to do a whistle-stop tour of the physical and political geography of Ireland. Maps are provided on the following pages for your reference. The overwhelming division is of course the north/south divide between the Republic of Ireland and Northern Ireland – a division which is primarily political in nature. The Republic is referred to variously as *Ireland*, *the 26 counties*, *the South*, *the Republic*, *Eire* (the Irish name) and *RoI*. Northern Ireland, on the other hand, can be described as *the Six Counties*, *NI* or *NoI*. In the Republic of Ireland, people typically refer to Northern Ireland simply as

Connacht

ATLANTIC
OCEAN

REPUBLIC OF
IRELAND

NORTHERN
IRELAND

0 ____ 50 km
0 ____ 30 mi

Donegal
Bay

Bundoran

Grange

Lough
Melvin

Broad
Haven
Bay

Belderrig

Ballycastle

Killala
Bay

Easky

Sligo Bay

Sligo

Manorhamilton

Mullet
Peninsula

Bangor
Erris

Ballina

Ballysadare

Colloney

LEITRIM

SLIGO

Lough
Allen

Ballinamore

Achill
Island

MAYO

Lough
Conn

Tubbercurry

Ballymote

Drumshanbo

Leitrim

Mohill

Curraun
Peninsula

Mulrany

Swinford

Charlestown

Carrick
on Shannon

Newport

Kilkelly

Frenchpark

Clare
Island

Clew
Bay

Castlebar

Kiltimagh

Westport

Inishturk
Inishbofin

Killary
Harbour

Murrisk

Partry

Claremorris

Ballyhaunis

Ballymoe

Tulsk

ROSCOMMON

Roscommon

Lough
Ree

Glennagevlagh

Ballinrobe

Dunmore

Clifden

Connemara

Corib

Lough
Corrib

Tuam

GALWAY

Maam
Cross

Ballinasloe

Bertraghboy
Bay

Galway

Athenry

Laurencetown

Galway
Bay

Loughrea

Killimor

Shannon

Portumna

Inishmore

Aran
Islands

Inishmaan
Inisheer

Gort

Lough
Derg

ATLANTIC
OCEAN

REPUBLIC OF
IRELAND

Northern
Ireland

Connacht

IRELAND

REGIONAL VARIATIONS

190

Leinster

Map labels:

NORTHERN IRELAND
NORTHERN IRELAND

REPUBLIC OF IRELAND

IRISH SEA

Dundalk
Dundalk Bay
Castlebellingham
LOUTH
Granard
Longford
Kells
Slane
Drogheda
Lanesborough
LONGFORD
Lough Ree
Ballymahon
Mullingar
Athboy
MEATH
Dunshaughlin
Rush
Trim
Ratoath
Swords
Lambay Island
WEST MEATH
DUBLIN
Athlone
Edenderry
Howth
Clara
KILDARE
Marlay Park
Dun Laoghaire
OFFALY
Tullamore
Rathangan
Naas
Enniskerry
Bray
Frankford
Blessington
Greystones
Banagher
Portarlington
Lough Tay
WICKLOW
Birr
Wicklow Gap
Rathnew
Port Laoise
Stradbally
Glendalough
Wicklow
LAOIS
Athy
Baltinglass
Rathvilly
Aughrim
Carlow
Tullow
Tinahely
Arklow
Urlingford
Ballon
Gorey
KILKENNY
CARLOW
Kilkenny
Bunclody
Bennetsbridge
Ferns
Callan
Graiguenamanagh
Enniscorthy
Thomastown
Clonroche
Ballyhale
Castlebridge
New Ross
WEXFORD
Wexford Bay
Wellington Bridge
Wexford
Kilmore Quay
Rosslare Harbour
Hook Peninsula
Saltee Islands
St George's Channel
CELTIC SEA

Shannon

LP
50 km
30 mi

Legend:

- ■ *An Gaeltacht* (Irish-speaking areas)
- ■ Leinster
- ■ Other provinces

Northern Ireland
IRELAND
Leinster

Ulster

IRISH SEA

North Channel

Rathlin Island

ATLANTIC OCEAN

NORTHERN IRELAND

REPUBLIC OF IRELAND

ANTRIM

DOWN

ARMAGH

DERRY

TYRONE

FERMANAGH

MONAGHAN

CAVAN

DONEGAL

Belfast

Derry

Cushendall
Ballycastle
Bushmills
Armoy
Portstewart
Coleraine
Kilrea
Moville
Carndonagh
Greencastle
Buncrana
Rathmullen
Milford
Creeslough
Dunfanaghy
Falcarragh
Bunbeg
Annagry
Glenties
Dungloe
Letterkenny
Ramelton
Strabane
Castlefin
Stranorlar
Donegal
Plumbridge
Newtownstewart
Omagh
Castlederg
Dromore
Belleek
Derrygonnelly
Enniskillen
Lisnaskea
Newtown Butler
Clones
Cootehill
Killeshandra
Butler's Bridge
Virginia
Ballyjamesduff
Ballyhaise
Shercock
Carrickmacross
Castleblayney
Kilroot
Armagh
Keady
Monaghan
Aughnacloy
Caledon
Auher
Fintona
Dungannon
Cookstown
Magherafelt
Maghera
Draperstown
Claudy
Limavady
Larne
Island Magee
Carrickfergus
Whitehead
Holywood
Bangor
Newtownards
Millisle
Greyabbey
Portaferry
Comber
Saintfield
Downpatrick
Newcastle
Castlewellan
Rathfriland
Warrenpoint
Newry
Dromore
Banbridge
Moira
Lisburn
Lurgan
Portadown
Craigavon
Markethill
Tandragee
Randalstown
Antrim
Ballymena
Kells
Newtown Crommelin
Ballyclare
Newtownabbey

Tory Island
Aran Island
Loughrea Peninsula

Strangford Lough
Carlingford Lough
North Channel
Camlough Bay
Bann
Lower Lough Erne
Upper Lough Erne
Lough Melvin
Trawbreaga Bay
Gweebarra Bay
Donegal Bay
Glen Gesh Pass
Mourne Mts

50 km

Northern Ireland
Ulster

IRELAND

An Gaeltacht (Irish-speaking areas)
Ulster (Republic of Ireland)
Ulster (Northern Ireland)
Other provinces

ATLANTIC OCEAN

REPUBLIC OF IRELAND

CELTIC SEA

An Gaeltacht (Irish-speaking areas)
Munster
Other provinces

the North. However, they don't usually mean the term to apply to the political region as such, but are merely referring to the geographical area (which happens to encompass the British province of Northern Ireland).

Another geopolitical feature of Ireland is the division of the island into four **provinces**. This goes back to late Gaelic times when the kingdoms of the old chiefs were divided into five territories known as **cúigí** (pronounced *coo·ig·ee*). The Irish word **cúige** (*coo·ig·eh*) literally means 'a fifth', as in a one-fifth part of Ireland. The five **cúigí** later became four provinces with the absorption of Meath into the province of Leinster. The four modern provinces of Ireland are given below with both their English and Irish names. The Irish translations prefaced with the word **Cúige** were used as a literary device and also by chroniclers of Irish history.

Connaught	*Connacht(a)/Cúige Chonnacht* – meaning 'Conn's land'
Leinster	*Laighin/Cúige Laighean* – meaning 'land of broad spears'
Munster	*An Mhumhain/Cúige Mumhan* – meaning 'land of Mumha's men'
Ulster/Ulaidh	*Cúige Uladh* – meaning 'land of Ulaid's men'

During Ireland's Golden Age (the period prior to serious attempts at conquest and colonisation by the Normans in the 12th century) the five **cúigí** were little more than loosely federated kingdoms with somewhat flexible boundaries. In their modern incarnation as provinces they've become associated with groups of specific counties, but these groupings are geographical entities that have never had any statutory basis under either English or Irish law.

Under the Anglo-Norman and British administrations, the four provinces gradually developed into 32 **counties**. Of these, 26 are in the Republic (hence the name *the 26 Counties* to refer to the Republic of Ireland) and six are in Northern Ireland. Subsequently, cultural and sporting bodies such as the *Gaelic Athletics Association* (*GAA*) organised their activities along county lines, and today they attract strong loyalties, particularly in the sporting field. County boundaries as they're popularly understood don't quite match the division of Ireland into administrative counties, however.

County nicknames

The 32 counties that make up the island of Ireland all have nicknames. These nicknames have either been passed down by history, bestowed by the locals, coined by the Tourist Board or (in the majority of cases) dreamt up by *Gaelic football* fanatics. The section below takes a look at county nicknames on a province-by-province basis with just a wee bit of general information about the provinces themselves thrown in.

CONNAUGHT

This is Ireland's western province, traditionally the most barren and wild part of the country (which in the old days was an economic bane and is now a tourist boon). Its main urban centres are Galway City in the south and Sligo Town in the north. Connaught is colloquially known by many, simply and affectionately, as *the Wesht*. Connaught was one of the ancient kingdoms of Ireland, whose rulers, the O'Connors, were supplanted by the Anglo-Norman De Burghs in the 13th century.

The Irish language is spoken in the *Gaeltacht* areas in the west of counties Mayo and Galway, the largest area being Connemara, one of the most beautiful parts of Ireland. In an effort to preserve its Irish-speaking status the local government recently ruled that only Irish speakers could get planning permission to build houses in Connemara.

Galway the ***Tribal County***. Galway City is known as the ***City of the Tribes*** and locals are known as the ***Tribesmen***. The tribes were 14 mercantile families who controlled the trade and politics of Galway City in the later Middle Ages and early modern period. The other name for locals, ***Herring Chokers***, owes it genesis to the fact that Galway is a maritime county and herrings have traditionally formed an important supplement to a diet of potatoes.

Leitrim the ***Wild Rose***; the ***Ridge County***. Wild roses are among the few things to grow profusely in County Leitrim. They're particularly numerous in the northwestern portion of the county. The name ***Ridge County*** refers to the method of growing potatoes in earthen ridges separated by ditches. This was done throughout Ireland but was particularly common in Leitrim.

Mayo the ***Heather County***; the ***Maritime County***. Heather covers much of the western portion of this western county. The ***Maritime County*** nickname comes from the fact that Mayo has one of the longest coastlines in Ireland.

Roscommon the ***Sheep Stealers' County***. Somewhat unfairly, Roscommon came to be associated with sheep stealing. Many of those found guilty and transported for the offence in the 19th century came from Roscommon. However, the practice may predate the 19th century. It was long ago noted that people from Roscommon 'borrowed' livestock from neighbouring counties, especially Longford and Westmeath, which are separated from Roscommon by the wide waters of the Shannon. In the days before proper communications and policing, property and theft were much the same thing.

Sligo ***Yeats' County***. The great Irish poet William Butler Yeats (1865–1939) spent much of his time in County Sligo and it inspired some of his finest poetry. He's buried there, in the churchyard of Drumcliff to the north of Sligo town. Inhabitants are jocularly known as **Herring Pickers**. Like inhabitants of maritime counties throughout Ireland, County Sligo residents augmented their food supplies with herrings that were easily caught from the shore.

LEINSTER

Leinster contains the capital of Ireland, Dublin. During the Middle Ages, the Kings of Leinster fought against the Kings of Meath. Its wealth and accessibility made the ancient province subject to both Danish and Anglo-Norman invasions.

Carlow the **Barrow County**; the **Dolmen County**. The River Barrow flows through the county and there's a large prehistoric monument or dolmen at Brownshill outside Carlow town. Residents are known as the **Scallion Eaters**, as much of the county is very suitable for growing scallions.

Dublin the **Fair City**, which comes from the words of the ballad *Molly Malone* – 'In Dublin's Fair City, where the girls are so pretty' etc. **Jackeens** is the colloquial name for Dubliners. The name reputedly derives from Jack/John Bull – a typical Englishman in Irish eyes in much the same way that a **Paddy** is a stereotypical Irish man – with the addition of the Irish diminutive *-ín* ending. There's also a tradition that it came from the Union Jacks that were waved enthusiastically by some Dubliners during royal visits. **Jackeen** is now used rather derogatorily for any Dubliner, especially one with a broad Dublin accent, and is the antonym of **culchie** (a country bumpkin). However, it may have been first used to denote **West British** Dubliners, or **Little Englanders** – both terms used to pejoratively refer to Irish people with loyalty issues.

Kildare the **Short Grass County**; the **Thoroughbred County**. Kildare is a county of rolling plains with grass kept short by munching thoroughbreds. A **GAA** name is the **Lillywhites**, because the County Kildare **GAA** jersey is all white.

Kilkenny the **Marble County** (Kilenny city is known as the **Marble City**). Much of the city, including its pavements, was built from locally mined marble. Kilkenny locals (and members of the Kilkenny *hurling* team) are called the *Cats*. The story behind this name is somewhat gruesome. During the British suppression of the 1798 rebellion, some German troops were stationed in Kilkenny. Being bored by barracks life they decided to make some entertainment by catching two cats, tying their tails together and suspending them from a washing line. The two cats naturally fought one another in a vain attempt at escape, much to the soldiers' perverse enjoyment. When their commanding officer appeared on the scene, the soldiers liberated the cats by cutting off their tails. When asked what had happened they replied that the bloody tails were all that was left after two Kilkenny cats had fought each other!

Laois *Queen's County; O'Moore County*. Laois was first raised to the status of a county by England's Queen Mary during the 1550s, and was named *Queen's County* in her honour. The O'Moores were the Irish clan who held most of the land in the area.

Longford the *O'Farrell County*; the *Country and Western County*. The O'Farrells were the Gaelic clan who controlled the land made into County Longford in the 1560s. For some unfathomable reason, country and western music is very popular in County Longford.

Louth the *Wee County* – on account of being the smallest county in Ireland

Meath the *Royal County*. The only county to have formerly been a kingdom. Also the seat of the inauguration site of the High Kings of Ireland.

Offaly the *Faithful County*. It's unclear where this nickname comes from but it's quite old. The motto of the county is *Esto Fidelis*, which roughly translates as 'keep the faith' in Latin.

Westmeath the *Lake County*. The county is home to many charming and a few reputedly dangerous lakes. Lough Rea (which it shares with two other counties) is reputed to have a monster lurking in its depths.

Wexford the ***Model County***. Progressive farming methods earned Wexford this title. The ***Strawberry Pickers*** is the name for Wexford locals, as Wexford is one of the few parts of Ireland where strawberries are grown on a commercial scale.

Wicklow the ***Garden of Ireland***. Wicklow's pleasant views were long regarded with pleasure by townscape-weary Dubliners, the first of whom to use the title was the poet Thomas More. Locals are named ***Goat Suckers***, as feral goats roam the Wicklow Mountains. There's an even less attractive variation on the name, ***Goat Suckers***, which implies that goats were used by some Wicklow men for more than mere milk.

MUNSTER

One of the ancient kingdoms of Ireland; control of Munster passed, after the Anglo-Norman invasion of Ireland, to the well-known families of the Fitzgeralds (Earls of Desmond) and the Butlers (Earls of Ormonde). Munster is the largest of the Irish provinces.

Clare the ***Banner County***. Political banners have been part of parades and events in Clare for a long time. The name probably goes back to the 1820s when ***The Liberator***, Daniel O'Connell, won a seat in Westminster from Clare but was initially unable to take the seat because he was a Catholic. O'Connell was very much the founder of modern Irish politics.

Cork the ***Rebel County***. The region is so named because it has often taken a position in major conflicts contrary to that of the former ruling British Empire and in opposition to British rule – many uprisings during the War of Independence (1919 to 1922) and the civil war occurred in Cork. The ***Rebels*** is the name of both the ***GAA*** and soccer teams. ***Donkey Aters*** (eaters) is the name attached to locals – one of the reputed reasons for the *Donkey Aters* tag is a belief amongst some that donkey meat is the real constituent of the Cork sausage delicacy known as *drisheen*. Cork City is regarded by many *Corkonians* as the *True Capital of Ireland* thanks to a haughtiness born of nostalgia, as in the 18th century Cork City was the commercial equal of Dublin.

Kerry the *Kingdom Kerry* or the *Kingdom of Kerry*, often simply abbreviated to the *Kingdom*. These monikers stem from the Irish name for the county, *Ciarraige*, which means Kingdom of Ciar, after Ciar, the progenitor of the O'Connor Kerry clan who took possession of the territory in AD 65.

Limerick the *Treaty County*. In 1690 Limerick City was the location for the signing of a treaty that ended the Jacobite rebellion in Ireland, and which promised the rebels free enjoyment of their lands and full civil rights. This was subsequently repudiated by the British. Limerick City is known, unkindly, as *Stab City* because of the allegedly disproportionate amount of violent fights there. The *Shannonsiders* is the name for locals as the city sits, one might say squats, astride the Shannon. This term is used for all local sporting teams.

Tipperary the *Premier County*; *Golden Vale County*. The *GAA* was founded in County Tipperary in 1884 which might be where the name *Premier County* comes from. As for *Golden Vale County*, the lush pastures (which, along with EU subsidies, allow the production of Irish dairy products) that run through part of Tipperary are called the *Golden Vale*. Tipperary locals are known as *Stone Throwers*. The origin of this is unclear but it just might have something to do with the Rock of Cashel, which according to legend was ripped out of a local mountain by the Devil but thrown aside because he didn't like the taste.

Waterford the *Crystal County*; the *Deise*. Crystal has been made in Waterford since the 18th century. The *Deise* is an old tribal territory in the area which, strictly speaking, only covers West Waterford.

ULSTER

This is Ireland's northernmost province, part of which (six of the nine counties) form Northern Ireland. The largest cities are Belfast and Derry/Londonderry (for an explanation of the slashed double name for this city see the Derry/Londonderry section, on page 203). Historically, the O'Neills and O'Donnells were the most powerful clans in the province.

Antrim (NI) *County of the Glens*. Antrim is home to nine *glens* (narrow and deep mountain valleys) referred to as the *Glens of Antrim*. Members of the Antrim *GAA* teams, especially *hurlers*, are called the *Glensmen*. The town of Ballymena is known as *Disneyland* because the Ulster Scots pronunciation of the contraction 'doesn't' comes out sounding like 'disney'. (Ulster Scots is a dialect of the Scots language spoken in Ulster; see Short History, page 17, for more on this.)

Armagh (NI) the *Orchard of Ireland*; the *Cathedral County*. Large numbers of apples are grown in Armagh. Armagh city is the seat of the Catholic and Anglican Primates of All Ireland, hence the *Cathedral County* tag.

Cavan (RoI) *Breffni County*. Most of County Cavan and a large part of County Leitrim formed the medieval kingdom of Breifne or Breffni.

Derry (NI) the *Oak Leaf County*. Derry comes from the Irish *doire* 'oak-tree'. The capital of the county is known colloquially as *Stroke City* (see the Derry/Londonderry section).

Donegal (RoI) the *O'Donnell County*; the *Forgotten County*. The O'Donnells were the Gaelic rulers of Donegal. The *Forgotten County* tag reflects that it's the furthest county from Dublin. Some benighted fools even think that it's part of Northern Ireland but it's actually part of Ulster province. Inhabitants are known as *Herring Gutters* because of the extensive coastline and prominent fishing industry.

Down (NI) the *Mourne County*. The Mountains of Mourne sweep down to the sea in the south of the county.

Fermanagh (NI)   the *Erne County*; the *Maguire County*; the *Lakeland County*. There are lots of lovely lakes of all sizes in this county, formed by the River Erne, which flows north through it. The Maguires were the leading Gaelic clan here – and don't call them McGuires – they're a separate crowd.

Monaghan (RoI)   the *Farney County*; *Drumlin County*. Farney was the name of an old medieval tribal territory. *Drumlins* are low but steep hills which characterise much of the landscape of County Monaghan and County Cavan.

Tyrone (NI)   *Tyrone Among the Bushes*; the *O'Neill County*, the *Red Hand County*. Lying in the heart of Ulster, Tyrone is one of the most beautiful of the inland counties, with the Sperrin Mountains in the north and well-wooded tracts in the south-east which gave rise to the frequently quoted tag: 'Tyrone among the bushes, where the Finn and Mourne run.' The O'Neills were the top dogs in Tyrone before the Brits moved in. The coat-of-arms of the O'Neills was a hand drenched in blood – though some insist it's just tomato ketchup.

Ulster political names

When it comes to the province of Ulster, it's not so much nicknames that cause confusion for outsiders but the language attached to the political and sectarian divisions that dominate life in the province. What follows is an attempt to shed some light on the local terminology – much of which is quite controversial. What should be obvious, though, is that language and politics are intricately intertwined in Ireland.

NATIONALIST NAMES

Nationalists in Northern Ireland and their supporters abroad most commonly refer to Northern Ireland as the *North of Ireland*. This implicitly denies British sovereignty over Northern Ireland by treating it as part of the rest of Ireland, at least at the level of everyday speech. This geopolitical anomaly confronts a host of paradoxical identities.

The Six Counties is another name popular among *Nationalists*, especially those extreme *Nationalists* who deny the legitimacy of the Republic of Ireland because it excludes Northern Ireland and who refer to the Republic variously as *the Free State* or *the 26 Counties*. *The Occupied Six Counties* is a phrase used by some *Republicans* to suggest that the British possession of Northern Ireland is illegitimate.

UNIONIST NAMES

Colloquially, the name *Ulster* has often been used (this is the Anglo-Norse version of the Irish *Uladh*, pronounced *oo·la*, combined with the Old Norse *ster*, meaning 'province'). It's a misnomer because *Ulster* includes nine counties – three of which are in the Republic of Ireland. The term was used officially in the title for the Northern Ireland police, the *Royal Ulster Constabulary* (otherwise known as the *RUC*), which has been superceded by the *Police Service of Northern Ireland*. It's also used in the name of the *Ulster Unionist Party* and the *University of Ulster*.

DERRY/LONDONDERRY

In a nutshell, *Nationalists* prefer to call the capital of Derry County *Derry*, while *Unionists* use *Londonderry* (retaining the prefix the city's name was given during the *Plantation of Ulster*). A suggested compromise wording, *Derry/Londonderry* (read as 'Derry stroke Londonderry'), has given rise to the local nickname *Stroke City* (not to be confused with the other use of the word *stroke* as slang for stealing!). Another method of partly circumventing this name problem is to write *L'derry* or *L-Derry*. Yet another way around the issue has been to refer to the city as *the Maiden City*, a reference to the fact that the city was not breached during the siege of 1689.

'H' FOR HOSTILITY

How you pronounce the letter *h* is a social marker in some countries, but it's traditionally been a sectarian one in Northern Ireland. Catholics generally pronounce it 'haitch', as do people in the Republic, while Protestants use the Anglo 'aitch' pronunciation. The letter *h* has therefore been the most dangerous letter in the Northern Irish alphabet, because if you were stopped and told to spell the word 'Henry', saying it in the wrong way in the wrong place could get you a Hiding (with a capital 'aitch' or 'haitch', depending upon what side of the fence your assailant was from).

Accents

Irish English accents – and there are an awful lot of them for such a small country – have all the traits of the typical *brogue* because they're all influenced by the vowels and consonants of Irish.

In some places, particularly in working class Dublin, speakers discard the final *t* of many words, so that 'brat' becomes *bra*, 'sweet' becomes *swee*, 'treat' become *trea* and so forth. The one you'll hear most though is *Wha?* instead of 'what?'. Said with a low pitch, this might mean 'I beg your pardon'. The higher the pitch and the more arched the eyebrows the more likely it is that it's an expression of incredulity, as in *A wha?* or *You're wha?*

The accent of the South, particularly down around County Cork, is the one most identify as the classic Irish *brogue*, and certainly the one closest to the *stage Oirish* that people tend to hear in bad Hollywood movies and try to mimic around the world. They'll often stretch words out and change intonation in the middle of a sentence so it sounds like three or four sentences in one. Kerry men and women, on the other hand, are prone to joining their words together and speak so fast that it sounds like they're almost singing. It's not karaoke, alas, so you'll really have to concentrate in order to understand.

West is pronounced 'west' everywhere except, well, in the West, where it's generally pronounced 'wesht'. If you're still with us, this anomaly is used in jest (or is that 'jesht'?) by the rest of the country for certain words like **stroke**, pronounced 'shtroke' in a cod-Irish accent to mean 'a political or other favour obtained through unofficial channels'.

Generally, the more rural your acquaintance the less likely you are to be able to understand them, particularly as they stretch out words like 'meat', 'eat' and 'beat' to become **maaate**, **aaate** and **baaate**. And they rarely drink water: it's **waher** without a t.

In the North (or 'Norn Iron' as it sounds in the local accent), they raise their intonation after a few words and then continue to the end of the sentence in the higher intonation. It gives a lovely lilt to what they say, but it can also be difficult to attune yourself to.

Generally, the Northern Irish accent bears some resemblance to Scottish English, with words such as 'book' rhyming with 'Luke'. Strange things also happen with vowel sounds in Northern Irish speech. Diphthongs (melded vowels sounds such as those found in the word 'boy') take on a different quality, giving Northern Irish that distinctive twang à la Gerry Adams.

Dialectical diversions

As Ireland's such a small country, there aren't many places where unique words and phrases can hide, so it's very common for the best slang and colloquialisms to travel around the country. You might hear the same things being said **all over the show** or **all over the shop** (everywhere). The various threads generally converge in Dublin, although the following are some homebody phrases that have been less keen to make the trip. We've attempted to group these words and phrases thematically – albeit loosely.

APOPLECTIC WITH RAGE

Don't get mad, get ... well in Cavan you might be *fit to be tied* while you could be *roarin'* in Offaly, *bullin'* in Limerick, have a *freaker* in Dublin or be *at the height of it* in Leitrim.

ARE YOU LEAVING?

You can't just up and go. You're *away* in Belfast, *gone* in Cavan, *heading off* from Dublin, *striking off* from Cork, and *legging it* from wherever the hell else you are (and usually in a bit of a hurry).

THE BOYS IN BLUE

The reason for your hurry isn't by any chance a run-in with law-enforcement officers, eh? They're *coppers* in Dublin, *peelers* in Belfast, *gyards* (pronounced *gee*·aards) in Cavan, *shades* in Cork, and *pigs* everywhere.

A GOOD JOKE

If it's very funny, they might *break their shite* or their *bollix* laughing in Dublin, *scitt* themselves in Limerick or *piss themselves* all over Ireland.

IDIOTS BEWARE

Don't be an idiot, or a *hallion* in Belfast, *a right wowlogs* or a *class of a clift* in Cavan. *Langers* come from Cork, *gobshites* from Dublin and *feckin' eejits* and *scalpeens* from all over.

IT'S NOT OVER UNTIL ...

There'll be no full stops until you say *so it is* in Belfast, *like* in Cork, *now* in Louth and *so* in Limerick, *right* (Dublin)?

NOTHING TO LOOK AT

If you're not exactly pretty to look at, Dubliners might say you *fell down the ugly tree* or are *no oil painting*. In Cavan they might say you've *a face like a monkey's arse*, in Limerick one that's been *kicked*. Elsewhere they might say *you've a head like a turnip* or you're *so ugly the tide wouldn't take you out*.

ONE TOO MANY

You might get drunk at home, but you'll get *tattered* or *half-cut* in Cavan, *langered* or *polluted* in Cork, *pissed*, *mickey monk* or just *bollixed* in Dublin, *scuttered* in Leitrim, *battered* in Limerick, *blootered* in Newry or *full* in Donegal. You could be *on your way* in Leitrim, but who knows what state you'll end up in if you go out *on the tear* (pronounced 'tare') in the North.

THE MADDING CROWDS

When crowds gather in Cavan, it's a *scran*. Dubliners are used to *a rake of heads* or somewhere being *black with people* (translated directly from the Irish *dubh le daoine*, pronounced *duv·le dee·nee*). If the group isn't to the person's taste, it might be called a *shower of eejits* or a lot worse (note: a *shower* is always used as a collective noun for an undesirable group). Around Kilkenny, you'll get a *hape* of people; *a lock* in Monaghan.

THINK YOU'RE TOUGH

See how macho you really are when you come up against a *hardchaw* in Dublin or *sham-feen* in Cork.

NUMBER ONE

When nature calls, you go for a *dreep* in Cavan, a *wazz* in Cork, a *slash* or *Jimmy Riddle* in Dublin, a *pump* in Down or to *drain the spuds* in Tipperary.

ROUND ONE

Don't get in a *row* in Belfast or you might get *lamped* or *clattered*. You'll get *belted* in Dublin, *pucked* in Limerick and *a tullock* in Cork.

WHEN YOUR BACK'S TURNED

They might not say it to your face, but in Dublin they'll have *a bitch* about you, they'll *read ya* in Limerick and *have a rag about* you just about anywhere.

DUBLIN STATUES

One of the most endearing qualities of Dubliners is their penchant for humanising statues, monuments and landmarks by giving them irreverent nicknames. As soon as a new one goes up there are dozens of contenders for the unofficial name, with the winner usually being incorporated into the local vernacular within months.

Unusually, the jury is still out on the 120-metre-high spire on O'Connell Street although *The Skewer in the Sewer*, *The Stiletto in the Ghetto* and *Milligan* (after the departed comedian, Spike) are all contenders.

In a nearby side street, Dublin's most famous son, James Joyce, stands with his cane and is fondly known as *The Prick with the Stick*.

Dublin's next most famous writer, Oscar Wilde, is depicted sitting on a rock in Merrion Square and is known unkindly as *The Fag on the Crag*. Nearby, poet Patrick Kavanagh is portrayed in contemplative mood alongside his beloved Grand Canal, sitting on *The Bench with the Stench*. Some call him *The Crank on the Bank* because he looks a bit intimidating when you just happen upon him.

Back across the *Sniffey Liffey* (Dublin's Liffey River), a bronze sculpture of two women sitting on a bench with shopping bags is better known as *The Hags with the Bags*. The Fair City's best-known woman, Molly Malone, can be found at the foot of Grafton Street, depicted with amazing bosoms and a wheelbarrow full of cockles and mussels. She is known, of course, as *The Tart with the Cart*.

Dublinisms

There are a couple of peculiarities in Dublin speech. Dubliners say *towen* when they're talking about the city centre. When Dubliners talk about *the rare oul' times*, they're referring to Dublin's version of 'the good old days' (as fondly remembered by older folks, who conveniently forget about all the whinging they used to do *back in the day*).

Belfast slang

Belfast, the second-largest city in Ireland, has some colourful slang of its own. If these expressions are delivered in that distinctive (and impenetrable) twanging accent you might have some trouble wrapping your ears around phrases such as these:

all day long	a general affirmation (roughly equivalent to 'certainly', 'yes', 'always' or 'a lot', depending on the context)
Am I some pup or what?	I'm feeling very pleased with myself
Catch yerself on!	stop talking nonsense
half gate	half of the agreed fee
hasn't a baldy notion	has no idea (how to do something), sometimes shortened to *hasn't a baldy*
keep her lit	keep your energy levels up; general words of encouragement
my bangers went	I lost my nerve
pluck	stolen or freely obtained goods
relax your cacks	there's no need to get stressed

sin é	(pronounced shin ay) Irish for 'that's it' used sometimes as a substitute for 'yes'
sliding	sneaking away
strap	credit
Suck the back of them!	you're talking nonsense and I am not going to do what you suggest
wee buns	that's very easy
wind your neck in/ pull your head in	don't get upset for nothing
you're a quare boy	you're some boy; aren't you great?

Cork talk

You know you've been in Cork too long when: everything's *grand, like*; you think Murphy's stout is *only savage* (cool; wonderful); you say *your man* and *boiee* (the local pronunciation of 'boy') in every second sentence; and you no longer eat anything cold, uncooked or not resembling meat, bread or potatoes.

CORK PLACE NAMES

Corkonians have a particular knack for renaming local landmarks. Nicknames for some of the most prominent sites to visit in and around Cork City are given here.

Clon	Clonakilty – a town in west Cork to the west of Cork City
Crosser	Crosshaven – also a town in west Cork to the west of Cork City

REGIONAL VARIATIONS

da Cross	Turners Cross Football Ground – holy ground for *The Rebels* aka Cork City FC (soccer) supporters and players; the holy-of-holies is *The Shed* (the covered terrace favoured by the fans)
Da Han	Ballyphehane – another Cork City suburb
da Peace Park	Bishop Lucey Park – opened in 1985 as part of Cork City's 800th birthday celebrations (named in honour of the long-serving Bishop Con Lucey of Cork)
Flying Bottle	the Holy Hill Inn – a popular pub (when Cork city do well and the boys are in a good mood, bottles and glasses fly through the air there!)
Grawn	Gurranabraher – a suburb of Cork's north inner city, once the home of 'real' Corkmen (ie working- and lower-middle-class folk), now being progressively gentrified
Knocka	Knocknaheeney – a suburb of Cork City
Mahn	Mahon – as above
Ovens	the name of this small town in County Cork is derived from the Irish word for 'caves'
Pana Sreet	Patrick Street – Cork City's crooked main street and the home of its finest shops (a great place for people-watching)
Toker	Togher – a suburb of Cork City on the south side between the centre and the airport

Origins of Irish place names

Every grid reference on a map of Ireland reveals something about Ireland's history, and every wrong turn on the road will tell you something about the various influences that have come to shape its unique place names.

Although the earliest place names were bestowed by pre-Celtic peoples, it was the introduction of Irish that had the biggest influence. The Norsemen also left their imprint, generally in the areas of the East and South that were preferred by the Vikings.

Whatever their origins, perhaps the most obvious influence on how the names sound today is the anglicised versions provided by the British. For example, Dublin got its name from a collaborative effort between the Vikings (who called it *Dubh Linn* 'black pool') and the British, who spelled it 'Dublin'. The Irish name for Dublin, **Baile Átha Cliath** (the Town of the Ford of the Reed Hurdles), actually refers to the settlement founded in 988 by High King Mael Sechnaill II which adjoined the town of **Dubh Linn** proper, at the Black Pool. (Although **Baile Átha Cliath** was never officially adopted as a name for the city, it appears on road signs and bus fronts.) Similarly, the town of Wexford was originally called *Weis Fjord* by the Vikings but was later anglicised.

The British began making detailed maps of Ireland in the 1830s. As part of this process, they needed to identify and delineate every **townland** in the country (a **townland** is the lowest-level geographical unit of land used in Ireland, smaller than a parish or county). Linguistic scholar and historian John O'Donovan is the man responsible for a great number of the official English names. With great diligence and empathy for Irish names he visited many parishes and places to research the original names and tried to stay as faithful as he possibly could to them when anglicising them. Phonetic versions of Irish place names were retained but they were officially given English spellings. Such was the case with the place name *Béal-fierste*, which means 'the mouth of the **lough**' (a **lough** is a long narrow arm of the sea), which later became Belfast.

BEYOND THE PALE

During the Norman era (from the 12th to the 15th centuries), the Normans tried to keep themselves separate from the Irish, and so their influence was largely limited to a walled area known as *the Pale*, roughly equivalent in size to today's metropolitan Dublin. What happened *beyond the Pale* was beyond their control and, to them, outside the bounds of acceptable behaviour and social convention, which is how the phrase entered the English language.

This process provided some very long place names, the longest being *Muckanaghederdauhaulia,* which clocks in at a mere 22 letters (to save you counting). The Irish version of this name is *Muiceanach idir dhá sháile* which means 'a marshy area between two saltwater inlets'. You can see from this example that four Irish words were strung together to make the English version of the word. Most place names in Ireland would, in fact, be two or three words if they were written in Irish. For example, Drogheda would be *Droichead Átha*, 'the bridge of the ford', and Mayo would be *Maigh Eo*, 'the plain of the yew tree'.

When new settlements were founded after English had become the main language, they were naturally given English names. Examples include places like Newtownabbey (County Antrim), Celbridge (County Kildare) and Lucan (County Dublin). There are fewer of these than you might expect given the length of time the British stayed at the helm.

When Ireland – or at least a portion of it – gained independence, the new government provided direct Irish translations for some English-named towns. For example, the County Kildare town of Newbridge, founded in 1816, was Gaelicised literally as *Droichead Nua*. Some other towns had their names totally changed: this was more common from 1922.

Anglicised versions of Irish words are incorporated into many Irish place names – often as prefixes. They evoke the distinctive geographical features of a given locality. The table on the next page gives the meanings of the most commonly encountered of these.

Irish word	Anglicised version	Meaning	Example
ard	Ard-	high, height	Ardagh; Ardeey
átha	Ath-	a river ford	Athlone; Athenry
baile	Bally-	a town or townland	Ballina; Ballybunnion
beag	Beg	small	Ballybeg; Lough Beg
béal	Bel-	mouth	Belfast
bun	Bun-	bottom or mouth of a river	Bunratty; Bundoran
carraig	Carrick-	a rock	Carrickfergus; Carrickmacross
cill	Kill-	a church	Kildare; Killarney; Kilkenny
cnoc	Knock-	a hill	Knock; Knocklong
dair	Derry	an oak grove or wood	Derry
druim	Drum-	a large ridge or long hill	Drumcliff; Dromore
dún	Dun-	a fortress	Dundalk
glas	Glas-	green in colour	Glasnevin; Glassan
gleann	Glen-	a valley or glen	Glendalough; Glendowa
inis	Inis-	an island	Inishowen; Inishmore
loch	Lough-	a lake	Loughrea
mór	-more	big or great	Inishmore; Dromore
rath	Rath-	a circular fort	Rathfarnham; Rathgar
sean	Shan-	old	Shankill; Shannon
tulach	Tulla-	a little hill	Tullamore

Throughout this book, a lot of reference is made to the debt owed by Irish English to its indigenous cohabitant Irish. Much of the unique flavour and beauty of Irish English – its lilting accent and its colourful vocabulary – is a direct result of the influence of Irish. With these points in mind, we've included this chapter to introduce to everyday spoken Irish, so that you get a feel for the language. This chapter will also help you to break through the barrier of the baffling Irish spelling system, by showing you how to pronounce words and phrases using our simplified pronunciation guides. In addition it will introduce you to some of the unique words for describing Irish life.

Another reason to familiarise yourself with Irish is that it's such a key part of Irish cultural identity. Against a background of repression and dispossession it's perhaps the fight to keep the native tongue alive that has best symbolised the desire to reconcile Ireland's cultural past – enshrined in song, stories, social traditions, folklore and dance – with its modern identity. While it's certainly true that a visitor to Ireland has no real practical need to speak Irish, having a go at it opens up greater possibilities of connecting with Irish people.

We begin our introduction to Irish with some facts about the language. Irish is the national and first official language of Ireland, and the ancestral language of the 70-million-strong Irish

AT A GLANCE ...

language name: Irish

name in language:
*Gaeilge gayl·*ge

language family: Celtic

key country: Ireland

approximate number of speakers: 1.5 million

close relatives: Scottish Gaelic, Welsh

donations to English:
brogue, cairn, clan, colleen, glen, shanty, shenanigans, slogan, smithereens, tory

diaspora, as well as most Scots, throughout the world. It belongs, together with Breton, Cornish, Manx, Scottish Gaelic and Welsh, to the Celtic branch of the Indo-European language family, once spoken across Europe from Ireland to Anatolia (modern Turkey). Irish and Scottish Gaelic shared a common literary language from the 6th to the late 18th centuries. The Latin word *Scotus* meant simply an Irish speaker, whether from Ireland or Scotland.

The Irish language helped inspire the movement that brought about Ireland's national independence in the early 20th century. It's been an obligatory subject at all primary and secondary schools since independence in 1922, and the number of Irish-medium schools has been rapidly growing in recent years. The study of Irish is a compulsory part of the **Leaving Certificate** (the final examination in the Irish secondary school system).

There are around 1.5 million Irish speakers in the Republic of Ireland and 140,000 in Northern Ireland. However, only about 400,000 claim to speak it on a daily basis. Irish remains the everyday language in the **Gaeltacht**, or traditional Irish-speaking areas, and is increasingly heard in urban areas, particularly in Dublin and Belfast. Irish is now broadcast on the Irish-language television station **TG4** and on **RnaG**, the Irish-language radio service. The language is also part of the European Union LINGUA program, a project which promotes the teaching of European languages throughout the member states. It's also one of the languages on the common EU passport.

An Gaeltacht (Irish-speaking areas)

Pronunciation

Stress almost always falls on the first syllable of a word in Irish. In our pronunciation guides, words are divided into syllables with the use of a dot and stressed syllables are italicised.

VOWEL SOUNDS

Vowels may be either short or long. In written Irish, long vowels are marked by a *fada* (resembling a French acute accent, eg ó). Irish also has a neutral vowel sound pronounced like the *a* in 'ago', represented here by the symbol uh.

Symbol	English equivalent	Irish example	Transliteration
Short vowels			
a	sof**a**	*cófra*	*koh*·fra
e	h**e**x	*te*	te
i	s**i**n	*inniú*	*in*·yoo
o	h**o**t	*tamall*	*to*·mol
u	p**u**t	*muc*	muk
uh	**a**go	*gorm*	*go*·ruhm
Long vowels			
aw	p**aw**	*amárach*	*a*·maw·rok
ay	h**ay**	*sé*	shay
ee	s**ee**	*mí*	mee
oh	r**o**pe	*cónaí*	*koh*·nee
oo	h**oo**t	*brú*	broo

Irish also has the following vowel sound combinations:

Symbol	English equivalent	Irish example	Transliteration
ai	**ai**sle	*saghas*	sais
ow	c**ow**	*domhan*	down

CONSONANT SOUNDS

Irish consonants are quite easy to pronounce as they all have equivalents in English.

Symbol	English equivalent	Irish example	Transliteration
b	box	*bos*	buhs
ch	cheese	*teach*	chokh
d	dog	*deich*	de
f	fun	*fuar*	foor
g	game	*gáire*	gai·re
h	hat	*thacht*	hakht
j	jump	*chairde*	khawr·juh
k	cat	*cat*	kot
kh	loch	*teacht*	chokht
l	let	*leanbh*	la·nuhv
m	meal	*mí-ádh*	mee·aw
n	naughty	*nocht*	nokht
ng	sing	*rang*	rang
p	put	*peil*	pel
r	run (but stronger, 'rolled')	*rí*	ree
s	sin	*scaoil*	skweel
sh	shell	*seacht*	shokht
t	tickle	*trí*	tree
v	vat	*bhí*	vee
w	wee	*Caoimhe*	kwee·ve
y	yes	*an dheisceart*	on yesh·kert

Numbers

1	*aon*	ayn
2	*dó*	doh
3	*trí*	tree
4	*ceathair*	ka·hir
5	*cúig*	koo·ig
6	*sé*	shay
7	*seacht*	shokht
8	*ocht*	ukht
9	*naoi*	nee
10	*deich*	de
11	*aon déag*	ay·en dayg
12	*dó dhéag*	doh yayg
20	*fiche*	fi·he
21	*fiche haon*	fi·he hayn
30	*tríocha*	tree·o·kha
40	*daichead*	doh·khod
50	*caoga*	kway·ga
60	*seasca*	shas·ka
70	*seachtó*	shokht·oh
80	*ochtó*	ukh·toh
90	*nócha*	noh·kha
100	*céad*	kayd
1000	*míle*	mee·luh

Time & dates

DAYS

Monday	*Dé Luain*	day loon
Tuesday	*Dé Máirt*	day mawrt
Wednesday	*Dé Céadaoin*	day kay·deen
Thursday	*Déardaoin*	dayr·deen
Friday	*Dé hAoine*	day hee·na
Saturday	*Dé Sathairn*	day sa·he·ren
Sunday	*Dé Domhnaigh*	day dow·nig

AROUND TOWN

city	cathair	ka·her
street	sráid	shrawd
town	baile	bo·lye
town square	lár an bhaile	lawr an bo·lye

MONTHS

January	Eanair	a·ner
February	Feabhra	fyow·ra
March	Márta	mawr·ta
April	Aibreán	a·brawn
May	Bealtaine	byowl·te·na
June	Meitheamh	me·hev
July	Iúil	ool
August	Lúnasa	loo·na·sa
September	Meán Fomhair	man fohr
October	Deireadh Fomhair	de·re fohr
November	Samhain	sow·en
December	Nollaig	nuh·lig

SEASONS

spring	an t-earrach	on ta·rakh
summer	an samhradh	on sow·ra
autumn	an fómhar	on fohr
winter	an geimhreadh	on giv·ra

TIME

hour	uair	oor
minute	noiméid	no·mayd
week	seachtain	shok·tin
month	mí	mee
today	inniu	i·nyu
tomorrow	amárach	a·maw·rok

Shopping

I'd like to buy (a) …
  Ba mhaith liom ceannach …   ba woh lum *kya*·nokh …
How much/many?
  Cé mhéid?   kay vaid

ornament	*ornáid*	*owr*·noid
photograph	*grianghraf*	*gree*·an·graf
picture	*pictiúr*	*pik*·toor
postcard	*cárta poist*	*kawr*·ta pwisht
shamrock	*seamróg*	*sham*·rohg
souvenir	*cuimhneachán*	*kwiv*·na·khawn
T-shirt	*t-léine*	tee·*lay*·ne

Meeting people

GREETINGS, GOODBYES & CIVILITIES

Hello.	*Dia duit.*	*dee*·a gwit
	(lit: God be-with-you)	
I'm …	*Is mise …*	is *mish*·a …
What's new?	*Cén scéal?*	kayn shkayl
Welcome.	*Fáilte.*	*fawl*·cha
Goodbye.	*Slán.*	slawn
Good night.	*Oíche mhaith.*	*ee*·ha wa
See you later.	*Slán go fóill.*	slawn go *foh*·il
Take care.	*Tabhair aire.*	toor *a*·ra
Take it easy.	*Tóg é gobogé.*	tohg ay go·*bog*·ay
Please.	*Le do thoil.*	le do hul
Yes/No.	*Tá./Níl.*	taw/neel
It is./It isn't.	*Sea./Ní hea.*	sha/nee ha

ON THE BUSES

Buses bound for the city centre have *An Lár* (Irish for 'city') on their signboards.

IRISH CURSES

Imeacht gan teacht ort.
i·mukht gon chokht urt
May you leave without returning.

Go n-ithe an cat thú is go n-ithe an diabhal an cat.
gu *ni*·he uhn kat hoo is gu *ni*·he an jowl uhn kat
May the cat eat you, and may the cat be eaten by the devil.

Titim gan eirí ort.
ti·tim gon *ai*·ree urt
May you fall without rising.

Thank you (very much).
   Go raibh (míle) maith agat.   go·ra (*mee*·luh) mo o·guht

You're welcome.
   Tá fáilte romhat.   taw *fawl*·cha roht

Excuse me.
   Gabh mo leithscéal.   gov mo *le*·shkay·al

I'm sorry.
   Tá brón orm.   taw brohn o·ruhm

How are you?
   Conas atá tú?   *ko*·nas *a*·taw too

I'm fine.
   Táim go maith.   tawm go moh

Very well, thanks.
   Go han-mhaith,   go *hon*·woh
   go raibh maith agat.   go ra mo o·guht

I'd like to introduce you to …
   Seo …   sho …

What's your name?
   Cad is ainm duit?   kod is *a*·nim dit

Pleased to meet you.
   Tá áthas orm   taw *aw*·has o·ruhm
   bualadh leat.   *bu*·la lat

MAKING CONVERSATION

Do you speak Irish?
An bhfuil Gaeilge agat? — on wil *gayl*·ge *o*·guht

Yes, a little.
Tá, beagán. — taw *byu*·gawn

How do you say that in Irish?
Conas a déarfá — *ko*·nas a *dyair*·faw
sin as Gaeilge? — shin os *gayl*·ge

I understand.
Tuigim. — *ti*·gim

I don't understand you.
Ní thuigim thú. — nee *hi*·gim hoo

Say it again, please.
Abair arís é, le do thoil. — *o*·bir *a*·reesh ay le do hul

Where's the toilet, please?
Cá bhfuil an leithreas, le do thoil? — kaw wil on *le*·ras le do hul

I'm/We're lost.
Táim/Táimid caillte. — tawm/*taw*·mid *kil*·che

Can you help me/us?
An féidir leat cabhair a — on *fay*·der lat *kow*·uhr a
thabairt dúinn/dom. — hurt *doo*·ing/duhm

WELL-WISHING

Cheers!
Sláinte! — *slawn*·cha

Long life to you!
Saol fada chugat! — sal *fa*·da *hu*·get

Health and wealth!
Sláinte is táinte! — *slawn*·cha is *tawn*·cha

Happy Christmas!
Nollaig shona! — *nuh*·lig *ho*·na

Happy Easter!
Cáisc shona! — kawshk *ho*·na

Bon voyage!
Go n-éirí an bóthar leat! — go *nai*·ree on *boh*·har lat

Meeting people

223

I disagree.		
Ní aontaím.		nee *ayn*·teem
You're right.		
Tá an ceart agat.		taw on kyart *o*·guht

Agreed.	*Aontaím.*	*ayn*·teem
What's this?	*Cad é seo?*	kod ay sho
What's that?	*Cad é sin?*	kod ay shin
Why?	*Cén fáth?*	kayn faw
Me too.	*Mise freisin.*	*mish*·a *fresh*·in
Neither do I.	*Ná mise.*	naw *mish*·a
Amazing!	*Dochreidte!*	*do*·khred·tye
How strange!	*nach ait é!*	nokh at ay
Impossible!	*Ní féidir é!*	nee *fay*·dir ay
Nonsense!	*Ráiméis!*	*raw*·maysh
That's terrible!	*Go huafásach!*	guh *hoo*·faw·sokh

BACKGROUND

Listed here are some countries where English-speaking travellers may come from. If your country isn't here, finding out how to pronounce the name of your country could be a good way of breaking the ice.

Where are you from?
Cad as duit? — kod os dit

Where do you live?
Cá bhfuil cónaí ort? — kaw wil *koh*·nee ort

I'm from ...	*Táim as ...*	tawm os ...
Australia	*an Astráil*	on *os*·traw·il
Canada	*Ceanada*	*kya*·na·da
England	*Sasana*	*sos*·a·na
Ireland	*Éirinn*	*ay*·rin
New Zealand	*an Nua-Shéalainn*	on *nu*·a·*hay*·lin
Scotland	*Albain*	*ol*·bin
the US	*Meiriceá*	*me*·ri·kaw
Wales	*an mBreatain*	an *mra*·tin
	Bheag	vyug

Do you have children?
An bhfuil páistí agat?   on wil *pawsh*·tee o·guht

Where do you work?
Cá bhfuil tú ag obair?   kaw wil too eg *ob*·ir

baby	*leanbh*	*la*·nuhv
brother	*dearthár*	*dri*·har
child	*páiste*	*pawsh*·te
daughter	*iníon*	*in*·een
father	*athair*	*a*·hir
grandfather	*seanathair*	*shan*·a·hir
grandmother	*seanmháthair*	*shan*·waw·hir
husband	*fear céile*	far *kay*·luh
mother	*máthair*	*maw*·hir
sister	*deirfiúr*	*dre*·foor
son	*mac*	mak
wife	*bean chéile*	ban *khayl*·uh

PLACE NAMES

Armagh	*Ard Mhacha*	ard *wa*·ke
Belfast	*Béal Feirste*	*ba*·le *fair*·shte
Clare	*An Clár*	on klawr
Cork	*Corcaigh*	*kur*·kig
Derry	*Doire*	*di*·re
Donegal	*Dún na nGall*	doon na nawl
Drogheda	*Droichead Átha*	*dri*·khi *aw*·he
Dublin	*Baile Átha Cliath*	*bol*·ye *aw*·ha *klee*·ya
Galway	*Gaillimh*	*go*·liv
Kerry	*Ciarraí*	*kee*·ree
Kilkenny	*Cill Chainnigh*	kil *ki*·nig
Limerick	*Luimneach*	*lim*·nok
Republic of Ireland	*Éire*	*ay*·re
Sligo	*Sligeach*	*slig*·okh
Tipperary	*Tiobraid Árann*	*ti*·brid *aw*·ran
Waterford	*Port Láirge*	port *lawr*·ge

Entertainment

GOING OUT

Yes, I'd like to.
Ba bhreá liom é.

bo vraw lum ay

Great, good idea.
Thar barr, an-smaoineamh.

har bor on·*smwee*·nev

I'm sorry, I can't.
Tá brón orm, ní féidir liom.

taw brohn *o*·ruhm nee *fay*·dir lum

INTERESTS

What interests do you have?
Cén caitheamh aimsire atá agat?

kayn *ko*·hiv *aym*·shi·re *a*·taw *a*·guht

What sports do you play?
Cad iad na cluichí spóirt a nimríonn tú?

kad *ee*·ad na *kli*·khee sport a *nim*·reen too

IRISH TRADITIONS

airneál	*awr*·nawl	an evening with storytelling by the fire
ceilí	*kay*·lee	a session of traditional dancing and music
gealgháirí	*gyal*·gaw·ree	a relaxed party atmosphere
seisiún	*se*·shoon	a traditional Irish music session

FESTIVALS

Bloomsday – June 16
James Joyce's novel, *Ulysses*, is celebrated through readings and dramatisations marking its hero Leopold Bloom's journey around the city of Dublin.

St Patrick's Day
March 17 is a national holiday, with parades held in Dublin and Armagh. The World Irish Dancing Championships also take place on this day.

World Irish Dancing Championships
About 4000 dancers from all over the globe compete in late March or early April. The location varies from year to year.

I like ...	Is maith liom ...	is mo lyum ...
basketball	cispheil	*kish*·fel
chess	ficheall	*fi*·khul
dancing	damhsa	*dow*·suh
football	peil	pel
Gaelic football	peil Ghaelach	pel *gay*·lukh
hiking	siúlóid	*shoo*·lod
hurling	iománaíocht	u·maw·nee·ukht
martial arts	ealaíona mílaeata	a·lee·na *mee*·lu·ta
movies	scannáin	*skan*·awn
music	ceol	kyowl
nightclubs	clubanna oíche	*klu*·ban·na ee·khe
photography	griangh-rafadóireacht	*green*·gra·fa·doh·rokht
reading	léitheoireacht	*lay*·haw·rokht
shopping	siopadóireacht	*shu*·pa·doh·rokht
skiing	sciáil	*skee*·awl
swimming	snámh	snawv
tennis	leadóg	*la*·dohg
travelling	taisteal	*tash*·tul
visiting friends	cuairt a thabhairt ar chairde	*ku*·irt a *too*·irt er *khawr*·juh
walking	siúl	shool

Food & drink

bread	*arán*	*a*·rawn
colcannon (potato dish made with leek and cabbage)	*cál ceannann*	kawl *kya*·nun
dessert	*milseog*	*mil*·shog
pie	*pióg*	*pee*·ohg
potato	*prátaí*	*praw*·tee
salmon and brown bread	*bradán agus arán donn*	*bra*·dawn *og*·as *a*·rawn don
soup	*anraith*	*on*·ra
stew	*stobhach*	*sto*·ukh
vegetables	*glasraí*	*glos*·ree
A drop of …	*Braon …*	brayn …
apple juice	*sú úll*	soo ool
beer	*beoir*	byohr
mineral water	*uisce mianraí*	*ish*·ke myee·an·ree
orange juice	*sú oráiste*	soo *or*·awsh·te
water	*uisce*	*ish*·ke
whiskey	*uisce beatha* (lit: water of-life)	*ish*·ke *ba*·ha
wine	*fíon*	*fee*·on

SIGNS

Céad Míle Fáilte	kayd *mee*·luh *fawl*·cha	A Hundred Thousand Welcomes
Dúnta	*doon*·ta	Closed
Fir	fir	Men
Gardaí	*gawr*·dee	Police
Mná	mnaw	Women
Ná Caitear Tobac	naw *kah*·ter *toh*·bok	No Smoking
Oifig An Phoist	*if*·ig on fwisht	Post Office
Oifig Eolais	*if*·ig *o*·lus	Tourist Information
Oscailte	*us*·kil·te	Open
Páirceáil	*pawrk*·awl	Parking

IRISH

228

WORDFINDER

A

B

G

M

R

S

X

Y

Z

INDEX